BOOKS BY TOM MILLER:

The Assassination Please Almanac

On the Border

Arizona: The Land and the People (ed.)

The Interstate Gourmet: Texas and the Southwest (co-author)

The Panama Hat Trail

Trading with the Enemy:
A Yankee Travels Through Castro's Cuba

Jack Ruby's Kitchen Sink:
Offbeat Travels Through America's Southwest

JACK RUBY'S KITCHEN SINK

JACK RUBY'S KITCHEN SINK

OFFBEAT TRAVELS
THROUGH AMERICA'S
SOUTHWEST

TOM MILLER

ADVENTURE PRESS

NATIONAL GEOGRAPHIC
WASHINGTON, D. C.

Published by the National Geographic Society
1145 17th Street N.W., Washington, D.C. 20036

The first draft of many incidents and episodes described in this book appeared in the following publications, more than half of which, I am chagrined to note, have since folded. *Arizona Trend, The Berkeley Barb, Cineaste, Crawdaddy, Hard Times, Hemispheres, The Nation, New West,* the *New York Times, Olé, Oui, Phoenix New Times, Nuestro, SunDance, Travel & Leisure,* and *Tucson Monthly.* Additionally, album notes from the Rhino Records release, *The Best of La Bamba.* "El Paso" by Marty Robbins. © Copyright 1959. Renewed 1987. Mariposa Music Inc./BMI (admin. by ICG). All rights reserved. Used by permission. "Felina (From El Paso)" by Marty Robbins. © Copyright 1966. Renewed 1994. Mariposa Music Inc./BMI (admin. by ICG). All rights reserved. Used by permission. Lyrics from "Open Pit Mine" reprinted courtesy GLAD MUSIC CO. © 1961 Glad Music Co. Finally, I am guilty of auto-cannibalism: I have drawn on material from two of my own books, *On the Border* and *Arizona: The Land and the People.*

First Printing November 2000

Interior Design by Gillian Carol Dean and Melissa Farris
Printed in U.S.A.

Library of Congress Cataloging-in-Publication Data

Miller, Tom, 1947–
    Jack Ruby's kitchen sink : offbeat travels through America's Southwest / Tom Miller.
    p. cm.
    ISBN 0-7922-7959-X
    1. Southwest, New--Description and travel. 2. Miller, Tom, 1947---Journeys--Southwest, New. 3. Southwest, New--Social conditions.
I. Title.
    F787 .M53 2000
    917.904'34--dc21

                                    00-048060

The world's largest nonprofit scientific and educational organization, the National Geographic Society was founded in 1888 "for the increase and diffusion of geographic knowledge." Since then it has supported scientific exploration and spread information to its more than nine million members worldwide.

The National Geographic Society educates and inspires millions every day through magazines, books, television programs, videos, maps and atlases, research grants, the National Geography Bee, teacher workshops, and innovative classroom materials.

The Society is supported through membership dues and income from the sale of its educational products. Members receive National Geographic magazine—the Society's official journal–discounts on Society products, and other benefits.

For more information about the National Geographic Society and its educational programs and publications, please call 1-800-NGS-LINE (647-5463), or write the following address:
NATIONAL GEOGRAPHIC SOCIETY
1145 17th Street NW
Washington, D.C. 20036-4688

Visit the Society's Web site at www.nationalgeographic.com.

To Regla

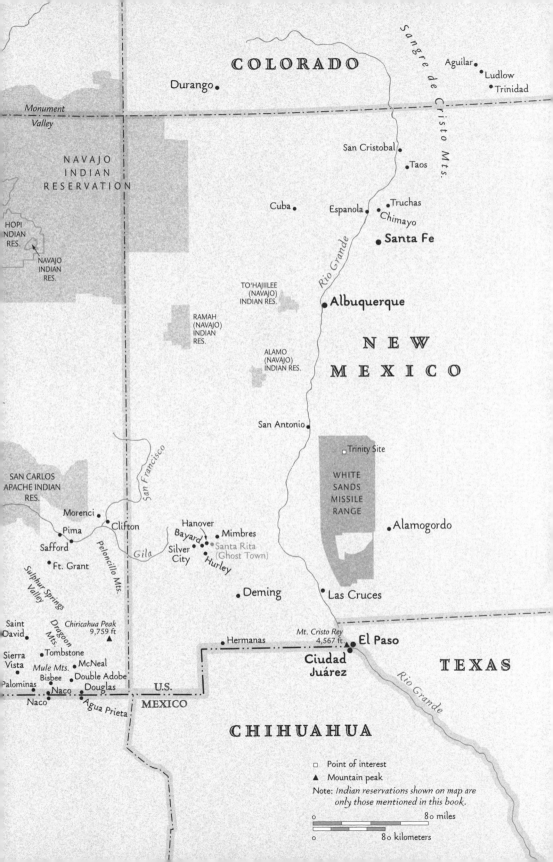

JACK RUBY'S KITCHEN SINK

CONTENTS

FOREWORD

～

Patrick Henry McCarty was just another wild kid in the Five Points section of New York in the early 1870s when he first heard the siren call of the American Southwest. The Five Points was the most disgraceful slum in the United States, dense with alcohol, poverty, drugs, and murder, and one fine morning the teenaged McCarty—as Huck Finn had in another context—decided to light out for the territory. He made his way to New Mexico, assumed the name of William Bonney, found work as a ranch hand and sheepherder, and ended up as one of the *pistoleros* in the famous Lincoln County War. He was soon called Billy the Kid, and supposedly bragged that he had killed 21 men by the time he himself was 21. He never did turn 22. Sheriff Pat Garrett gunned him down one July day in 1881, the same year that Henry James published *The Portrait of a Lady*. In a way, McCarty's early ending didn't matter. As Billy the Kid of the American Southwest, Patrick Henry McCarty had found immortality.

Billy the Kid was not the first Easterner to seek freedom and renewal by heading west. Although he almost certainly never heard of Horace Greeley, an obscure Brooklyn hoodlum named Alphonse Capone would make the same move 40 years after the death of Mr. McCarty. Alas, Mr. Capone decided to get off the train in Chicago, thus depriving the West of another golden legend. If only Mr. Capone had foreseen the development of air conditioning and the Federal highway system and the growth of passenger airlines, he might have beaten Bugsy Siegel to the glorious feat of inventing modern Las Vegas. Sometimes, life really is only a matter of timing.

Timing didn't diminish the reputation of Mr. Capone. Like Billy the Kid, he murdered his way into his own kind of immortality. Each of them lives on in books and movies, embraced by that inexhaustible segment of the American people that is thrilled by guns and sudden death and has never heard of Henry James.

Tom Miller is an Easterner, too, out of Washington, D.C. He found his way west during the late 1960s, that time in America when revolt was in the air along with a demand for renewal, both fueled by the music of rebellion. Young Americans were saying a collective No to the war in Vietnam. Parents were rejected, the suburbs were rejected, racism was rejected.

But that immense No also contained a very large Yes. The young, Miller among them, were trying very hard to make something new—that is, to establish values and social codes that were more humane, more open, more free. They talked about new ways of living. They started communes. They talked about the land. Some of it was foolish, much of it was adolescent, and a lot of it was touching and real.

The Yes played itself out in the American West. The East came to symbolize decay: physical decay, the collapse of industry and cities, the end of the immigrant myth. The migration into open places was an American migration, with millions of Americans leaving one version of the country and going to another. Tom Miller embraced the borderlands of the Southwest, as if sensing that his own subject matter lay in the buried templates of that beautiful, empty region that had once been Mexico.

He started writing for alternative newspapers, the many weeklies that grew up in the era in homage to—or imitation of—New York's *Village Voice*. Those newspapers defined themselves by attitude and tone. They made no pretensions to an impossible objectivity; that was a time, after all, for choosing sides. But they intensely covered those subjects that got scant (or clumsy, or baffled) coverage in the mainstream press: the anti-war movement, drugs, racism, feminism, music, and the people who lived on the margins of the so-called American dream.

Miller was somewhat different; he embraced the subject matter without adopting the furious tone. He was too good a reporter and too fair a man to fall easily into glib ideological ranting, substituting rhetoric for seeing. He loved the Southwest because of what it was, instead of what it was not. But he wasn't a booster out of the chamber of commerce either. He loved the border towns, from which Mexico had never departed, and celebrated their disorder and danger and tawdriness. He loved the austere pleasures of life in the desert. He loved places like Bisbee, the site of so many heartbreaking nights in the struggle to establish unions. And he wrote about those places with affection for the people who shared his own visions.

Later, when many of the young grew up and had children and moved on, Tom Miller remained in Arizona. He never accused those who gave up their youthful visions of selling out, that most terrible of 1960s sins. Too many of his contemporaries, shaped by the glancing power of television, learned only enough about a place to leave it. Miller was not so easily satisfied. He kept going around, as Murray Kempton once defined reporting, and learning something new, and writing it down. This book is about some of his discoveries.

On the surface, Miller's discoveries are not about what James Joyce once called "all those big words that get us in so much trouble." He can tell us about the origins of the song "La Bamba" and the creation of the chimichanga. He can find something worth knowing about the beginnings of paintings on black velvet and the obscure history of the bola tie. He can express his admiration for the late Edward Abbey, understand the man's rage and desire for desert solitaire, but he never embraces the worst of Abbey, who struck many people as insufferably self-righteous.

Miller can wander through the desolation of Mexico's Pinacate volcanic fields, traversed by hungry Mexicans heading for El Norte and drug smugglers working for big scores, and make you pray that nobody else decides to follow his reporter's path and the desert is left alone. He can also suggest the innate tragedy of a murder that crosses American generations in an American city north of the border. There is humor in Miller's writing, and sadness, and an occasional triumph. All those qualities can be found in the story of a lordly 125-year-old, 3,000-pound saguaro cactus that stood in the desert north of Phoenix, shot down by a drunken, beer-wrecked American bum who wanted target practice. The lout kills the great plant, but in a marvelous ending reminiscent of 10,000 Westerns, the plant gets its revenge.

In all of his work, here in this book and elsewhere, Miller has one other admirable quality: he refuses the fashionable. You will not hear him delivering sermons about globalization. You will not find him gripping crystals and facing some magical mountain, while aging white ladies chant New Age mantras. There is too much fun in the world for such nonsense, and besides, New Age culture can't be embraced by anyone with a sense of irony. Miller's ironies are reasonably gentle, and never savage. Anger over the spoiling of the land underlies much of his work, as it should anger any Americans who love beauty. But he always makes clear that his anger is not the subject. The place is. The place of beauty.

I did my own glancing year in the American Southwest, and learned what Billy the Kid never lived long enough to learn: I was shaped by cities, by noise and traffic and a thousand small daily collisions, and it was in cities that I belonged. That is, in my own city of New York, my native place. I live about seven blocks from the area that was once called the Five Points (now covered with Federal buildings and courthouses) and from which Patrick Henry McCarty began his journey into American myth. But the Southwest is alive within me, too, put there by movies and photographs and paintings, and by long drives under the naked moon. And I'm as possessive of it as anyone who lives there. I want to know that it actually exists, that there is a piece of my country where men talk to coyotes and paint on black velvet, and that if I feel the need, I can go to it the way I go to the Metropolitan Museum.

The *idea* of that distant place is not the exclusive property of those who live there. It belongs to me, too; it belongs to every American, including all those who might never pass through its austere amazements. In his work, Tom Miller has brought the region to life in his own special way, without donning the grouchy costume of what used to be called a "regional" writer. He is not defensive; he is

celebratory. He helps us all see beyond the ancient pulp fictions to the dailiness of life in that American place and in
doing so, he adds to its reality and magic. We should all
thank him.

—Pete Hamill
September 2000

INTRODUCTION

~

The contemporary Southwest has been shaped by three elements: the Western movie, the moving van, and the swamp cooler. The Western, as wrong-headed and false as it could be, by attracting Easterners; the moving van, by making the move affordable and practical; and the swamp cooler, by comforting the newcomer. Ever since the very first Western, Thomas Edison's *Cripple Creek Ballroom*, outsiders have thrilled to action and attitudes that simply never existed. Then the moving van made the impractical possible—allowed entire families and all of their possessions to venture into the unknown land of cowboys and Indians, pollen and pavement. And the swamp cooler—a marvelously simple invention that sucks dry, hot air through cool, damp straw to refrigerate a house—has made the unique American climate of the desert Southwest tolerable during its four insufferable summer months of hot, still air.

When friends back East ask what moving to the Southwest would be like, I begin by describing a photograph—easy to visualize—taken in Utah and Arizona's Monument Valley at the confluence of Hollywood and Madison Avenues, where some of the image industry's most evocative work has taken place. The myth, effortlessly exploited. In the photo's background, I explain, are magnificent mesas that appear as a movie set, too beautiful to be real; a U-Haul in the foreground sits idly by the side of a lonely two-lane blacktop, its passenger checking a road map. I continue to conjure the image for my listeners. It is a placid image, photographed by Mark Klett, simply composed, but my friends invariably express befuddlement. They do not seem to know if the scene I'm describing is admirable or if I am mocking. Am I touting the natural wonders of the region or disparaging the disoriented newcomer? Does the scene enthrall me or do I accept its implicit discord?

MARK KLETT (WET-PLATE TECHNIQUE)

Crossing from Utah into Arizona in Monument Valley

I plead guilty to all of the above. I never tire of the land in the American Southwest, am invariably dubious of man's efforts to use or improve upon it, and am always ready to explore and exploit the tension this creates. To the Northeast, the Southwest is exotic, the "other." The imbalance of this polarity attracts newcomers, which further aggravates the imbalance. I aggravated this imbalance by moving to the Great American Southwest in the late 1960s, knowing nothing about either the land or its people. I lived back East, and daydreamed through that window in one's early adulthood when neither job nor classroom nor family nor love battens one down. Until then I had ventured no farther west than a line from Chicago south to Dallas. I yearned to get as far as I could from the East Coast—without getting to the West Coast. Ultimately I jumped through that window and landed in Tucson. All that my friends and I knew about Arizona at the time was that Barry Goldwater and marijuana both came from there, and I thought that any place that could simultaneously sustain both would indeed be intriguing.

I wrote for the underground and the rock press then, and was gratified to find an active antiwar movement and low-profile counterculture firmly in place. As a writer who took part in the events that I covered—what was later called the "participant-journalist"— I enjoyed a 360-degree mobility into those worlds. Not long after arriving in the Southwest, I had an opportunity to carry this out when I arranged for the Dusty Chaps, a longhair country-rock band that played original tunes as well as Merle Haggard and Faron Young covers, to entertain at the Safford Federal Correctional Institution. Safford, a minimum-security prison, housed white-collar criminals, draft resisters, and Mexicans who had crossed the border illegally once too often. We were bringing aid and comfort to our troops, a sort of USO show for conscientious objectors.

A short time after I wrote up the Safford show, two-year-old San Francisco-based *Rolling Stone* called: "Can you drive over to Taos this afternoon?" an editor asked. "The hippies on the Lower East Side are headed that way this summer. We need a piece on what they can expect when they get to northern New Mexico." It proved a reasonable assignment once I informed him that Taos was 650 miles distant and I couldn't get there that afternoon. A few years later, having expanded the range of publications I wrote for, I heard from an editor at *Esquire*. He wanted coverage of an event in Texas, and asked if I could—I believe these were his exact words—"mosey on over to Houston for a day." I informed him that if we both started moseying at the same time, he'd likely mosey into Houston before me.

Initially ignorance and misconceptions about the Southwest bothered me, but I soon learned their source and history. "Lying about the West in general and the Southwest in particular," writes author Charles Bowden, "has been an American cottage industry for over a century." And one, I discovered, in Central Europe as well. Karl May, a German writer, wrote stories about the American West that featured valorous and admirable Indians. *Winnetou,* his best-known series, began in the 1870s and was as wildly inaccurate as it was popular. The three volumes about an Apache scout so captivated the German reading public's imagination that to this day they hold Karl May festivals, reenact Indian gatherings, conduct May-oriented excursions to the American West and Southwest, and continue to practice a somewhat guileless but entirely genuine devotion to

Native Americans and all that they symbolize. *Winnetou* and other May adventures, published in dozens of languages, are among the best-selling fictions of all time. Herman Hesse and the Alberts Einstein and Schweitzer were big fans of his. May resolutely established the classic image of the West in the European mind; it was a land of tepees and cowboys on the receding frontier.

A German "reenactor," or Berlindian

Not that it mattered to his millions of fans, but Karl May did not visit the American West until long after his Westerns were complete. And although his writing, curiously, has never been embraced in the United States, its pastoral, late 19th-century romanticism of the Noble Savage tinged the popular notion many Americans still hold of their own West. Yet if Winnetou himself were alive today, he would likely be the greeter at an Indian casino.

"The Southwest still exists upon realities," wrote noted author Paul Horgan in 1933, "instead of symbols of realities." Today, myths that endure in the Southwest are the ones worth dissecting, deconstructing, and, when warranted, dismantling. Replacing them is harder, and writing about them can be challenging, but it is often this mythology that draws me deeper into the region and inspires my writing. It motivates me to explore the unexpected twists of events and the fierce emotions that both provoke and sustain the Southwest's enduring legends. There is no substitute for researching a historical incident at the very spot it took place, suggested author Barbara Tuchman; it is how you acquire the all-important "feeling of the geography, distances, and terrain involved." The difference between radical travel and conventional travel is simply how much you inhale along the way.

We all endure hardships in the Southwest, large and small, whether we moved here from elsewhere or know no other region. Earnest assurances to the contrary, a Chicago native will never be completely satisfied with the pizza here; likewise a New Yorker with the bagels. The poet Luci Tapahonso, a member of the Navajo Nation, complains that finding good mutton off-reservation is impossible as close as Albuquerque. Culinary borders can be as real as any other sort, and like the others we must accept them while hoping to find our way around them. A border implies the end of a territory; a frontier intimates the land beyond. They both crisscross the Southwest, and the daunting task can simply be to understand them both. "One place comprehended," Eudora Welty has noted, "can make us understand other places better."

The Southwest, now subsumed under the commercial rubric of the Sunbelt, has watched much of its identity snatched away by advertising and suffocated by urban explosion. "The growth of the Sunbelt has altered our perception of our landscape," author Rudolfo Anaya observes. "The old communities, the tribes of the Southwest, have been scattered, and they have lost much of their power." This process began in the mid-19th century when, with the spoils of the Mexican-American War, our national saddlebag fairly overflowed with two-thirds of Mexico. Anglo colonists were encouraged to travel to the new territories; they brought with them the ability to ring a cash register and quickly developed the talent to run cattle.

The dynamic that this created has not yet reached an equilibrium, and fortunately the Southwest's quiet, romantic qualities are still with us. It is through this shifting balance that I invite you to travel the Southwest and dip into neighboring Mexico with me.

—Tom Miller
Summer 2000

CHAPTER 1

THE GREAT STINKING DESERT

Nothing happens all the time in the Sierra del Pinacate. This region of extinct volcanoes, lava flows, and sand dunes, covering more than 600 square miles just beyond the Arizona border in Sonora, Mexico, supports little life and less industry. Throughout history, hunters, smugglers, and missionaries have walked the Pinacate floor; writers, artists, and soothsayers have sung its praises. Traces of Indian life from the first millennium have been found just beneath its surface. Astronauts destined for lunar voyages have trained in its craters. Earth must have looked like the Pinacate before man evolved, and I imagine Earth will again resemble this haunting and seemingly infinite land when no one remains to appreciate it.

The Sierra del Pinacate embodies some of North America's most striking contemporary themes: wilderness exploration, space travel, environment, contraband, nature's delicate balance, immigration, and solitude. In the course of my occasional wanderings there by foot and truck I have uncovered shining exemplars of them all.

When I first visited the Pinacate in the mid-1980s, the region fell under the jurisdiction of a Mexican bureaucracy seemingly too stingy to maintain the land's pristine qualities. It was a staging ground for illegal foot and contraband air traffic, a feature that has changed only somewhat. Longtime Pinacate junkies—for the most part, an agreeably ornery bunch of weathered scientists, adventuresome artists, and hard-core campers—fear that more visitors there will forever damage the delicate landscape and ruin their magnificent and eerie turf. The Pinacate beetle, *Eleodes armata,* which when threatened stands on its head and gives off a slightly foul odor, provides both the region's name and perhaps the best

Near Elegante Crater in the Sierra del Pinacate, Mexico

perspective from which to view this unfriendly land. Militant naturalist writer Edward Abbey, a man intimate with inhospitable desert land, described the Pinacate terrain as "the bleakest, flattest, hottest, grittiest, grimmest, dreariest, ugliest, most useless, most senseless desert of them all."

Fernando Lizárraga Tostado, the Pinacate's one-man ranger-caretaker-policeman-host-naturalist for most of the 1980s, appreciated the capricious relationship man has had to the land here. He worked for a Mexican ministry that appropriated less money for maintaining the Sierra del Pinacate than the U.S. National Park Service allotted for toilet paper in its adjoining land. Back then Fernando told me his bosses took away the trailer that housed his family and office, and he seldom got enough gas money to top off the tank in his pickup.

For many years an American group gave informal aid to ecological causes in Mexico, including efforts to protect the Pinacate. The organization, Friends of ProNatura, gave a camera to Fernando as well as a two-way radio, typewriter, gas money, and data on bighorn sheep that roam back and forth between Mexico and the United States. After years of agitation from naturalists, wilderness advocates, and environmentalists from both countries, in 1993 the Mexican government declared the region a Biosphere Reserve, part of which lies within the Patrimony of Humanity— a UNESCO program that makes funds and preservation possible— in the Upper Gulf of California. Officially, the land is called La Reserva de La Biósfera de El Pinacate y Gran Desierto de Altar, and it includes the Sierra Blanca range to the south and the sand dunes closer to the Golfo de California on the west.

Fernando, in plaid shirt and brown trousers, invited me into his pickup after we met for breakfast in the Mexican border town of Sonoyta. "To use the Pinacate," he instructed as we headed down the highway, "you must know the rules: The park is not closed to the public, but you have to register with me." Even then, visitors were restricted to Cerro Colorado and Elegante Crater. Before using the land, visitors had to sign the Pinacate Pledge: "I am aware of the established rules and promise to promote conservation of this marvelous open-air museum." Under a new system gradually implemented in the late 1990s, Mexico's Ministry of Ecology and Natural Resources has opened a visitor's center and set up picnic tables at designated campgrounds. With more elaborate and explicit rules regulating noise, pets, hiking, cooking, and alcohol, the guidelines boil down to this: Behave yourselves!

Eventually Fernando and I drove south in his battered, muddy Chevy pickup, down narrow roads lined with clumps of creosote bushes and small paloverde trees. In the western distance, two low volcanoes interrupted the desert flatness. Fernando pointed out the tracks of some bighorn sheep. "The sheep—they're illegal to capture, but we have hunters who come in here and shoot them for sport. They just want them for trophies. Someday they'll be in danger of completely disappearing. For many years the hunters had an orgy of blood here."

Lizárraga pointed to Celaya, a volcanic mountain he boasted was "rich in human history." A little bit farther on he stopped the truck not far from Celaya and motioned me to follow him on foot. We stood near a slightly shaded area just above a dry natural water tank. "A long time ago an Indian community lived nearby," he said, referring to the Hiac'ed O'odham, better known as the Sand Papago. More immediate to Fernando, though, was that for decades a Tucson archaeologist named Julian Hayden had come to the

Pinacate and knew the contours of its land better than any other human. "I call this spot 'Julian's Fireplace.' He stays here when he comes. He's here for a day and a half and then he leaves. He talks to the coyotes, Julian does. He has good conversations with them! When Ron Ives died"—Ives was among the first modern scientists to study the region—"Julian tossed his ashes off the top of a hill near here. I want to erect a plaque here marking 'Julian's Fireplace.' We call him 'El Burro Viejo.'" A picture of the Old Burro hung prominently on the wall of Fernando's home. After El Burro Viejo died in 1998 at age 87, some of his ashes were spread near Julian's Fireplace.

Back in the truck we passed some kids kicking around a soccer ball at a few shacks that make up an *ejido*—a government-designated community on cooperatively tilled land. "They farm alfalfa, wheat, and cotton," Fernando explained. "At least when there's rain. And when it comes, it's sudden. The sky darkens and the ground gets drunk."

A few miles farther on we saw a couple of ragged men tending some goats. "There's another ejido here, but it's just a small operation. That little area"—we drove past a few ramshackle buildings by the road—"that's Papalote. Illegals cross there up into a big arroyo on the U.S. side. From there they go to La Paloma, a ranch west of Organ Pipe," the 516-square-mile national monument in Arizona just north of the border.

Poachers arrived soon after Highway 2 was paved in the 1950s. They hunted, they set up clandestine mining operations, and they carted away ironwood trees. The wood made good furniture and even-burning fires—and, they figured, it wasn't doing anyone any good wasting away in El Gran Desierto. Depleting the Pinacate's ironwood forest disrupted different food chains, including that of the bighorn sheep, who munch the leaves of ironwood and other trees for survival. When the poaching of ironwood trees by colonists became frequent in the mid-1980s, Fernando once confronted some poachers and switched from affable naturalist to authoritarian cop: Surrender your settlement documents, he reportedly ordered, or you'll see the army next. The men had Fernando outnumbered and outgunned, but they gave up. At one point he was actually paying squatters not to cut a particularly large ironwood tree.

Just off the highway Fernando spotted tire tracks on a new, unauthorized dirt road heading back to a supposedly abandoned cinder mine. Cinder mining—illegal in the Pinacate—involves processing small cinder particles built up into cones that result from volcanic eruptions. The cinder itself finds commercial use as blocks and other construction material. Fernando checked the tracks, then talked with a tired old man we found sitting beneath a lean-to he had made from the nearest building material, the ribs of dead cactuses. "We have problems with unauthorized trails. I'll have to call headquarters about this."

Soon we arrived at the home of Pablo, a spry 71-year-old who lived next to a clandestine cinder mine, which operated only a few months of the year. In season, the cinder from Pablo's mine was trucked north across the border to a construction company in Phoenix. Pablo, the off-season caretaker for the mine's foreign owner, was at this particular moment fixing his lunch. A grandson

50 years younger lived with him in a spare two-room shack with chickens and a dog underfoot. Pablo was delighted to have company and rambled on about his life and wives.

"Heh-heh, I like the young ones. I'm a *robaverde*. How do you say that in English?"

"You're robbing the cradle," I suggested.

Fernando unloaded two oil drums filled with water, enough to last Pablo until his next visit the following week. As we left, Pablo returned to flipping tortillas above his ironwood-powered stove.

∾

Inspiring absolute feelings is the timeless strength of the Pinacate; few other natural settings can claim this. The first outsider to travel through the Pinacate, Padre Eusebio Kino, established Jesuit missions in the late 17th and 18th centuries throughout the Pimería Alta region, in what are now the states of Sonora and Arizona. The natives, he noted, wore scraps of rabbit fur and ate insects, roots, and fish. Looking southwest from the top of one mountain in the Pinacate range, Kino saw the Golfo de Califronia and Baja California beyond. He is credited with ascertaining that Baja California is a peninsula rather than, as previously imagined, an island.

Authors such as Zane Grey (in *Desert Gold),* Louis L'Amour (*Last Stand at Papago Wells),* Jeanne Williams (*A Lady Bought with Rifles),* and Kristin Michaels (Williams's pen name, *The Magic Side of the Moon*) have drawn on the starkness of the land and the power of the sun to invent dramas involving cowboys, Indians, and tall, dark strangers.

The two best books to capture the Sierra del Pinacate are old and obscure. The first, *Camp-Fires on Desert and Lava,* recounts zoologist William T. Hornaday's remarkable 1907 foray from Tucson into the heart of the Pinacate. The other, *Campos de fuego* ("Fields of Fire"), came out in 1928. Written by Gumersindo Esquer, a Sonoyta schoolteacher, it begins as a fairly credible book about a spur-of-the-moment trip into the Pinacate by a bunch of convivial folks but soon develops into a wild sort of psychedelically inspired Mexican science fiction.

Hornaday, who traveled with eight compatriots under the auspices of the Carnegie Desert Botanical Laboratory, commented that although the area was known to a few Indians and Mexicans, "to the reading and thinking world, it was totally unknown." After traipsing southwesterly to a border crossing, the party made it into Mexico: "To be rain-soaked on our first day in el desierto of Sonora, and thoroughly chilled also, was like being prostrated by heat in Greenland; and wondering what would happen next to us unexpectedly, we thankfully devoured a shameless meal, and crept into the snug comfort of our sleeping bags."

Hornaday and his crew named a crater after one of their own, Godfrey Sykes, who dutifully measured the height of each mountain climbed, the depth of each crater descended, and the diameter of each volcano hiked. "You seem to stand at the gateway to the hereafter," Hornaday wrote of Sykes Crater. "The hole in the earth is so vast"—almost 750 feet deep—"and its bottom is so far away, it looks as if it might go down to the center of the earth." Another volcano, Hornaday wrote, "was like Dante's Inferno on the half shell."

Zoologist Hornaday's specific mission was to gather data about animal life in the Pinacate, a task he carried out with increasing bloodthirstiness. He and the others started off with solemn vows to kill sheep only for meat, but as their time in the dry-heat wilderness passed, the author—also a taxidermist—rationalized killing after killing, insisting that each was intended for a museum. Then he'd retreat into righteousness: "The sheep of the Pinacate could easily be exterminated in three years or less, by the Mexicans of the Sonoyta Valley for meat, or by the scores of American sportsmen who are willing to go to the farthest corner of Hades itself for mountain sheep."

Campos de fuego, the extravagant Mexican science fiction, leads the reader from ground level, where the troops spy a lion, into a mile-long underground cave, a virtual city with bronze images of Christ and skulls, "which appeared to belong to a race of giants." By attaching their tents to cactus ribs, the group parachute to the bottom of a crater, where they discover a crevice, behind which a passageway leads them into a labyrinth of underground tunnels and an abyss, "which it seemed would take us to the center of the earth."

Both Hornaday and Esquer alluded to an underground life, and no wonder—the most volatile activity takes place below the earth's surface, not above it. The peaks are not tall by any standards—the highest stands only 4,235 feet above sea level—and the surface, for the most part, lacks shade and water. The mountains were formed when the earth retched up ash and rock and flame. And that is the secret source of the Pinacate's power: Its tremendous energy comes from underground, rather than from all that later metamorphosed on its surface.

~

Few people have made practical use of the Pinacate region—legal, anyway—because it offers so little other than primitive camping and mental cleansing. It resembles the moon and it leads to hell. With the former in mind, Alan B. Shepard, Jr., and four other NASA astronauts came here in early 1970 to train for the Apollo 14 lunar flight. They could not have picked a more appropriate spot. They brought their Module Equipment Transporter—a hand-pulled cart nicknamed Rickshaw—and studied the remarkable geologic features the Pinacate offers. The astronauts' trip to the region has never been a secret, but it has never been publicized, either.

Using word of mouth as our guide, Tucson astronomer Bill Hartmann and I set out one blistering hot day to find NASA's needle in the Pinacate haystack. We were searching for a rock, rumored to be on the lip of a particular crater, where the moon-walkers literally left their mark. We each picked an area to search. I took a westward strip within 50 feet of the lip itself; Hartmann looked on the next hundred-foot outer ring. The rock we sought was said to be virtually flat, distinguished from a thousand other similar rocks only by scratches etched upon it decades earlier. The futility of the search was matched only by the lack of anything else to do. This was the only pinball machine in town. After a while my enthusiasm waned, and the foolish optimism I had brought to the task decreased with it.

Bill backtracked over my section while I wandered aimlessly looking elsewhere.

"Here it is!" Hartmann shouted. "Here's the rock!"

I ran over. There it rested—a table-top rock of weathered basalt with a dark brown desert varnish. It read:

NASA 2/16/70

APOLLO 14

and the name Hilda. Hilda's identity should be left to the imagination; likewise the location of the rock, for NASA's rock symbolizes the unity of the core of the earth, the surface itself, and the sky beyond. It links the Pleistocene epoch of a million years ago with space travel. At that spot deep in the Sonoran Desert, nature and technology are married.

I won't tell you where it is. If the site of the NASA rock were revealed, someone would roar through the Pinacate from the south in an ATV, which is strictly prohibited, and dig it out to smuggle back into the United States. I will tease you with this, however: The crater nearest the rock is named for the secretary of Mexico's Departamento de Fomento at the time of William Hornaday's trip.

~

I was unprepared for how protective the handful of Pinacate buffs would be when they learned I'd be writing about their land. They all spoke of the region's nakedness, its vulnerability, its virginity. The Pirates of the Pinacate, as I came to call the regulars, reminded me of a warning made by Daniel MacDougal, the botanist on Hornaday's journey: "If you enter the deserts to study them, go in a receptive and tolerant frame of mind or do not go at all."

"I'd hate to turn the public on to the Pinacate," one of the pirates said. "It's already so fragile." Another guardedly showed me a large pot she had found, intact, on her annual camping trip. "The sand had been blowing over it for centuries. A little bit of it was sticking up, and we kept on digging. Very carefully. I knew in an instant what we had found." An archaeologist has dated the pot from the 1300s, the days of the Sand Papago. A photographer no longer exhibits his pictures of the Pinacate, so fearful is he of enlarging the handful of Pinacate buffs: "The people who go there care." Another desert rat simply clammed up when I asked his favorite campground. You'd think I had demanded the number of his Swiss bank account.

In a way, I had. After a few trips into the Sierra del Pinacate I sensed the source of their fears and the treasure they hoarded. On the floor of one sandy and rocky crater, I was surrounded by bunches of saguaro and ocotillo cactus and clusters of mesquite and creosote. Looking out from the rim of another crater, it seemed a holocaust had struck Earth and this was all that remained. From a rugged hillside I turned to find the source of distant thunder cutting through a land awash in silence: A dozen bighorn sheep were galloping eastward across the desert floor. From my elevation I was able to follow their graceful strides for miles. Never have I seen air so extravagantly clear, so brutally still.

Most of the Pinacate's rattlers, vultures, and javelinas have never confronted shotguns, Nikons, or Jeeps. It reminded me of the volcanic Galápagos Islands, whose animals are likewise innocent of our imperial tendencies. Slabs of shimmering lava lie about the sides of some Pinacate volcanoes; barrel cactus, which the sheep break up with their hooves for moisture, spring from cracks in the rocky soil. Above ground, it is the Great Stinking Desert at its greatest and most stinking. New Mexico artist P. A. Nisbet speaks of "atmospheric clarity" and "a magical sense of deep space" when describing the Pinacate. The range, he says, "has the character of mystery and the quality of darkness about it. It's primeval, terrifying, and reassuring at the same time. You feel as if you're walking through the Pleistocene age."

The pirates' protectiveness was understandable; elitist antagonism was something else. Soon after returning from one of my trips, a call came in from out of state, quite unsolicited, from a man I didn't know. He had heard through the grapevine that I hoped to write about *his* Pinacate for a weekly newspaper. "It's a sacred place, and it shouldn't be revealed to common street people," his tirade began. "I don't see any reason to draw attention to that area. It has a pristine quality, but you can sense the deterioration with each additional visitor. Last time I went I didn't see another human for an entire week. I had 360-degree open vistas the whole time. Yellowstone, Yosemite, the Grand Canyon—they're just amusement parks compared with the Pinacate. I've made 50 trips there over the past ten years. Most people who go there now are true explorers or geologists or anthropologists—scientists who have a love for the desert. If not another person were to find out about the Pinacate, except by his own personal exploration, well, that'd be fine. It's one of the last strongholds of the Sonoran Desert."

The pirates, of course, are further bothered by the more recent and better organized administration. "It's hard to get around now," one told me. "I've seen the Mexican army and American DEA in there. All the back roads and most of the campgrounds are now prohibited. It's riskier to move around." In other words, it ain't what it used to be.

At night, northbound planes loaded with drugs have taken off from old airstrips originally built for mining operations. One of the Pinacate pirates told of running into armed men in a truck near nightfall on the western side of the Sierra, but he didn't stay around long enough to learn their activities. Not far from there I picked up a Mexican hitchhiker in his 60s whose face itself somewhat resembled the floor of the Pinacate, weathered and dry with sudden outcroppings. He said he lived on the outskirts of the range and confirmed what I'd been told up till then. "Oh, yes, of course, marijuana and cocaine cross there. I've seen the landing strips. But I don't think they send a lot across at a time. It's just too isolated."

At the northern edge of the Pinacate, tongues of jagged lava called aa (a term from Hawaii, where they speak volcano) stop just shy of the U.S.-Mexico border. Mexico Highway 2 parallels the border, and Mexicans hoping to enter the United States often travel along the highway at the edge of the Pinacate before turning north into the unmerciful desert. Now and then too much heat and too little water leaves them deader than Hornaday's sheep.

Three truck stops along the Pinacate's northern expanse are considered takeoff points for smugglers called coyotes shepherding Mexicans and others into the United States. The café-gas station at Los Vidrios seems to get all the attention. Word among the pirates was that since the long-time owner sold the business to some strangers, it has been taken over by drug smugglers. One of the pirate kings said he refused to stop there any more—"Can't tell who or what you'll run into." Another pirate, researching the splendid bighorn sheep, was a bit apprehensive when I suggested we go to Los Vidrios.

"Why don't you just tell me about it afterward, okay?"

Any builder would be proud to claim Los Vidrios as his own creation. The three-building complex is made entirely of volcanic rock so solid and settled that it resembles a fortress more than a café. A water tower constructed of the same rock, filled three times a month with water trucked out from Sonoyta, sits in back. The Sierra del Pinacate is Los Vidrios's front yard.

When I stopped by, a few truckers sat sipping beer while their rigs were prepped outside. Gimme caps filled part of one wall—from a furniture company in Mississippi, a construction outfit in Massachusetts, and one from Mr. Steak, address unknown. An unused wood-burning stove sat in the corner. Gas lanterns replaced electrical lights a few weeks earlier when the power went out. Owner Alberto Soto Acosta came up to wait on me. "We don't have a menu," he said, "but you can order whatever you want. You can even get huevos rancheros at two in the morning if you'd like. Carne machaca is the most popular dish we serve." Soto's elderly relatives busied themselves in the kitchen. His wife lived in Phoenix. "She's an immigrant. I don't have papers."

A truck filled with cabinets arrived from the central state of Michoacán; as the driver and his family unloaded them to sell in the parking lot, I asked Alberto about the Pinacate. "Oh, sure, I've seen bighorn sheep. But I've never gone across the highway to explore." We walked around back of the café and looked into the United States. "People cross here, not contraband. The smuggling is closer to the cities. The wetbacks come in groups of anywhere from four to twelve. Mojados—U.S.-bound migrants—pass by from Oaxaca and Tabasco and other states where there's real high unemployment. Usually they'll stop and ask for water and food before they start out. The last group of four left a few days ago—all they had was a little container for water. It wasn't enough. A galoncito."

Soto motioned to the desert floor northwest of the café. "Rattlesnakes live there. Once we found some bones in that direction. We never knew if the person died from dehydration or from the rattlers."

The biggest problem at Los Vidrios, which means pieces of glass, has nothing to do with smugglers or contraband. It's jets from Luke Air Force Base. "They fly overhead," Alberto said, "and sometimes the windows break. We often feel the tremors. The whole house shakes," a motion he demonstrated with his body. Though their airspace ends at the border, the pilots above, like the migrants below, often don't recognize the international border.

The best-known visitors to Los Vidrios have been Juan Matus, a Yaqui sorcerer better known as Don Juan, and Carlos Castaneda, the writer who chronicled Don Juan's powers. In June 1968, with Castaneda at the wheel and Don Juan riding shotgun, the two stopped for a bite at Los Vidrios on their way to a peyote ceremony, according to *A Separate Reality*. Looking into the Pinacate at night from his table at Los Vidrios, Castaneda saw "black jagged peaks...silhouetted against the sky like huge menacing walls of glass slivers." He assumed this was how the truck stop got its name. Don Juan replied that the name came from glass shards lying around the highway for years after a truck carrying glass had overturned there.

Following their meal, Don Juan noticed Castaneda feeling a bit queasy. "Once you decided to come to Mexico," Don Juan admonished, "you should have decided to put all your petty fears away." After pulling out to the east, Carlos looked in his rearview mirror and saw what appeared to be headlights gaining on him. Don Juan knew different. "Those are the lights on the head of death," he said. When Castaneda looked again, the headlights had vanished. Death had turned south into the Sierra del Pinacate.

WHAT IS THE SOUND OF ONE BILLBOARD FALLING?

Ed and I sat in a fire tower above Aztec Peak, a 7,748-foot-high mountain in Arizona's Tonto National Forest. Slowly he stood up, grabbed a half-full carton of sour cream, walked outside the lookout tower, and heaved it far into the forest below. The container rested near the top of a tall ponderosa pine. The sour cream glopped down to lower branches and finally to the ground as a couple of Los Angeles television producers slowly pulled out of sight. It was Edward Abbey's way of wishing them Godspeed down the treacherous dirt road to the paved highway.

In the publishing industry, Abbey was categorized as a "Southwest writer," a condescending but ultimately benign label that plagues those writing about the area west of Louisiana and east of Los Angeles. More than a decade after his death in 1989, Abbey still has what is euphemistically called a "cult following," which simply means that devoted readers enthusiastically spread their admiration by word of mouth, thumping dog-eared paperbacks in front of friends who haven't yet fallen prey. His words are sufficiently safe for classroom reading lists, incendiary enough to trigger fury against public works, and adequately anarchistic to dispense with polite discussion. His fictional characters sometimes assumed cartoon qualities and their dialogue could be clunky, but his appeal transcended literary niceties for sturdy truths. Notwithstanding the fact that one of his books was made into a movie—*The Brave Cowboy* became the Kirk Douglas classic *Lonely Are the Brave*—and despite having written one of the great books of the American Southwest, *Desert Solitaire,* Abbey's notoriety never broke through the invisible barrier separating "underground following" from popular acceptance.

Lord knows he tried. The subject about which he was most eloquent and prolific—wilderness preservation—became, as he put it, "in vogue," and for a number of years he was at the height of fashion. Still, "wilderness preservation" sounds too much like the tail end of a preachy bumper sticker. Abbey made defiant celebration of the outdoors without yielding to the "ain't it beautiful" approach. He stood apart from others by his cantankerous and acerbic style, mocking land exploiters and tepid liberals in the same phrase. He could go for pages describing something as common as a sunset and never lose the reader. Joyful veneration of the natural world coupled with defiance of man-made strictures permeated his writing, an attribute that distinguished Abbey from others. It was this virtue that made him a most reluctant guru to environmentalists, and it was this quality that spurred the men from the television network to visit his mountaintop summer home.

The 16-by-16-foot room at the top of a 50-foot-high metal tower afforded him a hundred-mile view in all directions. In addition to living essentials, the glass-enclosed lookout perch, which resembled nothing so much as a prison guard tower in a World War II movie, contained the tools of his trade: an Osborne fire scanner, detailed terrain maps, an intercom linking him with other lookouts, binoculars, and gauges to measure rain, temperature, and humidity. On occasion he saw elk in the meadow west near the Peterson Ranch; whitetail deer were common sights east toward the Murphy Ranch. More than once he spotted black bear at the bottom of his tower. In the upper reaches of Aztec Peak he could pick wild blackberries along a two-mile mountaintop trail, which has since been officially christened Abbey's Way. Like his writing, it has switchbacks and meadowland.

His workday four months of the year went something like this: Up with the sun at about five o'clock, down the 52 stairs to the outhouse and to shower—a bucket of cold water over the head—a run with his black Lab, Ellie, then back upstairs to intermittently play the flute, read, and sit and think. During what he called office hours—7 a.m. to 6 p.m.—he sat in a high wooden swivel chair in the southeast corner of the room, jotting in his journal. He listened to jazz, classical music, and Willie Nelson with one ear while the shortwave radio sputtered into the other. He was a man at peace. When the peace got too dreary, he walked to the other end of the room to pick up his binoculars and venture out onto the catwalk surrounding his home. He peered intently into the woods in all directions and returned inside, muttering. "Dammit, still haven't seen any raging forest fires. What a bore." He watched a peregrine falcon fly by at eye level, then started up in his journal once again.

On this particular day at Aztec Peak, Abbey could see foul air some 30 miles from the lookout tower. He radioed a co-worker: "Signal Peak, this is Aztec. I'm seeing an incredible amount of smog out your way. Where's it all coming from?" They agreed it came from Phoenix. Abbey appreciated the work he had carved out for himself. Jobs like this allowed him to buy time and, in lean years, food. In 1978 he sucked on his pipe and looked for puffs of smoke in the distance for $3.50 an hour. "I've got a job that requires very little intelligence. The waiting list is very long."

If backpackers or other strangers ventured near the mountain-top, he would lock the outhouse—"so I won't have to clean up after them"—and shut the trap door separating the uppermost flight of stairs from the catwalk encircling his room. He was by himself at the top of the mountain and generally preferred not to have uninvited guests climb up to his home to take in the magnificent view. An *Esquire* photo of Robert Redford camping along Utah's Outlaw Trail in snow-white cowboy boots provoked him to laughter; a *National Geographic* article about a woman's trans-Australia journey brought muttered jealousy. "I have no use for natural photography. I like photographs of places, animals, and people for history and documentation. But rivers and mountains and flowers—there's no use for it. I can't stand the stuff." I mentioned to Abbey that once shortly after I returned from a trip to northern New Mexico, still radiating from the glory of the

Sangre de Cristo range, I could finally grasp how some people get religion. "You don't understand," he insisted, "those mountains, that land—you don't *get* religion from them. They *are* religion."

His best writing illuminated that theology. If his works have a unifying theme, it is a simple, familiar one: Nature—the land beyond the land we know—battles capitalism, unrestricted access, industrial tourism, and rank abuse. You win some, you lose some. A "Jeffersonian anarchist" (his own label), Abbey described himself in a magazine piece as "beer-bellied, broken-nosed, overweight, shakily put together, with a bad knee [skiing accident]." He was grizzly and whimsical, well-read and inquisitive, drawing irony from a position he cheerfully conceded somewhat elitist. He bewildered his occasional college lecture audiences by spouting poetic pornography and bawdy environmentalism. It came as no surprise when the network producers reported back that Abbey was too unpredictable to consider for a national news feature. He could be a violent and offensive writer.

At the end of a rigorous day of vainly searching for forest fires, playing his flute, and writing, Abbey radioed in his final weather report. "I like that sunset," he said as he clicked off the two-way. "It's sinister-looking. Almost grim." His life was marked by writing, river-running, contemplation, and mountaineering through the backlands—and even this, he feared, was too ritualistic. "I must do some traveling. I've been hiding out in the desert. I've got to get out and see the world again. I haven't planned to do that since I lived in Hoboken." The night I spent with him was just brisk enough to warrant a light blanket and, as 360-degree lightning provided a silent and constant obbligato, I slept in Abbey's summertime studio as soundly as I have ever have slept in my life.

Seclusion such as this inspired Abbey's celebrated 1968 work, *Desert Solitaire,* a powerful and sensitive narration of a year in the Utah and Arizona wilderness. The book presaged the environmental movement, hence it is clear of all the claptrap that has bogged down much of the literature of ecology since then. It expresses a pure and occasionally lusty passion directed at the land, its users and abusers. And it thrust upon him a pack of loyal followers, devotees who created the demand for his lyrical and self-deprecating writing.

"I am slightly uncomfortable in this role," he admitted when pressed. "I'm not a 'naturalist leader' or any other kind. I'm a writer. I was writing about all this before it was popular, and I probably will when it's no longer topical. I don't want to write about the environment forever, but I don't know how long it will be a subject everyone wants to read." He gestured to a recent issue of *Outside* magazine. "Besides, when someone is willing to pay me a thousand dollars to write about why a road shouldn't be paved into a national park, it's hard to resist. Eventually I'd like to settle down and do novels. I really consider myself more a writer than an environmentalist." There was a thoughtful pause, then a sheepish grin. "Well, I guess I am an environmentalist. There's really no way around that."

Edward Abbey was born in Home, Pennsylvania, when Calvin Coolidge was still president. While slightly older friends were off fighting World War II, 17-year-old Ed Abbey took off by thumb, bus, and rail to see what lay far beyond the Alleghenies, to satisfy "that westering urge." His introduction to the Southwest was an arrest for vagrancy in Flagstaff, Arizona, a city that remained an occasional foil for his literary conceits. Except for a two-year stint in the army and a couple of years as a welfare worker in New Jersey, Abbey made the West his permanent home, sometimes wandering away, always returning. The National Park Service and the United States Forest Service employed him sporadically for more than 20 years. During his last decade, he taught nonfiction writing and juggled a schedule of traveling, further wilderness exploration, and writing.

One novel that he wrote atop Aztec Peak was set in post-industrial Phoenix. The city had been largely abandoned and civil war was raging: "simple anarchists and farmers" on one side, the military and reconstructionists on the other. The book followed the same theme developed in his other works, notably *The Monkey Wrench Gang,* his most popular, in which a merry band of ecoteurs plots to destroy Glen Canyon Dam. The construction of this dam along the Colorado River of Utah and Arizona created artificial Lake Powell, forever drowning some of the most spectacular and inaccessible canyon land in the country, a wilderness region dear to Abbey's heart and typewriter. In *The Monkey Wrench Gang,* published in 1976, environmental absolutists down billboards, sabotage earthmoving equipment, and lay elaborate plans to destroy the dam itself, restoring the Colorado River and Glen Canyon to their natural state. Few could rationally argue with that goal.

Eco-raiding was a skill not foreign to Abbey, and one that he wrote about with the leer of the sensualist. "I like civil disorder and natural disaster," he said one day, and we toasted public uproar and organic catastrophes over a hamburger lunch. "That's why I like storms, earthquakes, and mail strikes. It breaks things up; there is temporary disarray. Anything to disrupt the order. *The Monkey Wrench Gang* got people going. I'd get letters from people endorsing the idea of blowing up Glen Canyon Dam, asking how they could help. The dangerous ones would enclose detailed diagrams of just how to do it, complete with sketches telling me where to place the dynamite. They'd want to meet at clandestine sites to make plans." About all the brouhaha that book inspired, he remarked, "What's that Waylon Jennings line— 'Don't you think this cowboy bit done got out of hand?'"

~

In the 1950s and early '60s, Abbey read the works of William Eastlake, especially his Western trilogy, *Go in Beauty, The Bronc People,* and *Portrait of an Artist with Twenty-Six Horses.* Eastlake's writing, as would Abbey's in the following decade, had developed a loyal following: Arpad Gonz, later his country's president, translated *Portrait of an Artist with Twenty-Six Horses* into Hungarian. Writers from Jim Harrison to the late Kathy Acker praised his work. A fan underwrote the publication of an unfinished manuscript. One small press brought out an annotated bibliography, listing everything ever written by or about Eastlake.

Eastlake was convinced that Tom Robbins, Richard Brautigan, and even Ken Kesey had copied his style. He took praise well.

His books were a curiosity at first for their unusual portrait of the West. Pulp novels, shoot-em-ups, and B Westerns thrived at drugstore paperback racks and first-run movie theaters. But Eastlake's West was clever, literary, and droll. His cowboys stumbled and hankered for electricity and V-8s. They shaved from the same basin as Garrison Keillor's Lefty and Dusty. His fictional Indians were funny, occasionally duplicitous, always clever, and unfailingly amused by pitiful whites. They had names like President Taft, My Prayer, Walking Across a Small Arroyo, Jesus Saves, and Henry Three Ears of an Elk. They could roll a perfect cigarette in one hand without taking their eyes off you. Said one, "Well, at least I didn't go to Yale." Eastlake's Indians were neither noble nor savage.

The novels built Eastlake a steadily growing reputation for their simultaneous ability to entertain the critics and debunk the West, and by 1961 younger authors were seeking him out, Edward Abbey among them. At age 34, Abbey and the poet Robert Creeley drove a Volkswagen bus and a bottle of Old Crow from Taos down to Cuba, New Mexico, to the W Lazy E Bar Ranch, where Eastlake lived with his then-wife Martha. Creeley, who had written Eastlake his first fan letter six years earlier, thought him like Hemingway but with a sense of humor. For Creeley and Abbey, both goateed, this was their first meeting with Eastlake. The three spoke little of literature and lots of land. Eastlake saddled up his quarter horse Poco Más, turned the reins to Poco Menos over to Abbey, and gave Elegante to Creeley. The three writers rode through the high Chihuahuan desert until they reached Eastlake's herd, grazing illegally in a national forest. This impressed Abbey.

Edward Abbey (left) and William Eastlake

Abbey returned to Eastlake's land often and, as he described it, "one cold gloomy afternoon in November, we rode out to attempt to again find his cows." The two horseback writers became separated, and when a blizzard dumped layers of snow on New Mexico, their vision was cut to ten yards. Eastlake made it back to the ranch house; Abbey, realizing he was lost, gave his horse free rein, but Poco Menos was mucho perdido. A fire was out of the question; "I figured if things got bad enough," Abbey said later, "I'd open my knife and eviscerate the horse, keep my hands and feet warm in his smoking gut." When the storm ended around midnight, Eastlake trudged out, sporadically firing his shotgun in the air, hoping that Abbey would hear. After Eastlake had traveled a mile from his house, Abbey heard his shots and the writers reunited, with Poco Menos intact. The two forged a strong bond, Bill and Ed, one that held up through numerous books, bottles, wives, and zip codes.

Eastlake and I came to know each other quite by chance. I had moved to Arizona in 1969 and used my thumb to get around. One sunny December afternoon Bill pulled his tan pickup over to give me a lift. He touched the brim of his cowboy hat as I got in, leaned over, and shook my hand. "Eastlake," he said, introducing himself. "Not Westlake; Eastlake. E-a-s-t-l-a-k-e." As we drove down Speedway Boulevard, E-a-s-t-l-a-k-e was delighted to learn his passenger wrote for the underground press; he himself had just published an anti-Vietnam war novel, *The Bamboo Bed*. A couple of months earlier a local jury had found an Air Force sergeant named Palacios not guilty of the cold-blooded killing of a couple of hippies, and the Manson gang had just been arrested in California. Eastlake cautioned me against the wave of anti-longhair sentiment sure to follow. As he dropped me off near my house, he invited me out to his place at the base of Mount Lemmon for horseback riding and dinner the following weekend.

William Eastlake, born in Brooklyn to British parents, came West in the 1930s when he hitchhiked through New Mexico and Arizona to Los Angeles. There he worked at a bookstore on Hollywood Boulevard, meeting author Theodore Dreiser in his final years, the playwright Clifford Odets in his youth, and a host of Hollywood hacks in their prime. In that era, he later recalled, "I couldn't spell, and typed like a wounded man." After World War II, in which he won a Bronze Star, Bill and Martha kicked around Europe; in the 1950s, they moved to New Mexico, where they embraced ranching. Bill wanted to write about a part of the country neglected in serious fiction. To him the West meant excitement and remoteness, beauty and strangeness. He had in mind Walt Whitman's West: "The great American promise."

With the publication of *Castle Keep*, which prefigured Robert D. Hooker's *M*A*S*H* and other black looks at combat and its futility, Eastlake's reputation broadened from "Western writer"—first cousin to the "Southwestern writer"—to that of a worldly author who could blend burlesque, sharp dialogue, and morality. The Ford and Rockefeller foundations gave him money; *Portrait of an Artist with Twenty-Six Horses* won a prestigious award in France, where it was published in a distinguished series alongside Malcolm Lowry and Jorge Luis Borges; magazines asked him to write for them; universities in California and New Mexico invited him to be their "writer-in-residence." It was just such an offer from the University of Arizona that had coaxed Eastlake to Tucson, to our fortuitous meeting on Speedway Boulevard and our subsequent afternoon on horseback and evening around the dinner table.

Eastlake kept his horses stabled on a rural road surrounded by as much desert as you would want to ride through. We must have ridden an hour or so without spying a paved road. I do not recall my horse's name or its color; what I do remember is how proper and natural Bill Eastlake looked in the saddle, a combination of his British heritage and his Westerly countenance. In the faint distance we heard the front-porch cowbell peal, Martha's proclamation that dinner would soon be ready. By the time we got back to the house, Martha—a fellow writer who had written a cookbook called *Rattlesnakes Under Glass*—had steaks waiting. Rumors abounded that she did far more to her husband's manuscripts than simply type and copyedit them; indeed, after their divorce in 1971 his writing lacked its former literary snap.

Eventually Bill moved to Bisbee, a small and comfortable mined-out copper town near the Mexican border. When Ed Abbey made his occasional visit to his longtime friend down in Cochise County, the two would end up sitting near the pool table. They'd speak of crops, rain, cattle, and integrity; sipping, brooding, wondering.

Only once did a discordant note break through their harmony. At Bisbee's Copper Queen Hotel bar one winter night in 1983 a small group of us shared a pitcher with them and the talk drifted to immigration and the border. Abbey said he opposed "the Latino invasion of our country," and Eastlake responded with a facetious suggestion that the U.S. and Mexico effect a land swap. "Where were you, Bill?" Abbey challenged Eastlake the following day, still fuming over his friend's diffidence.

Usually they mused: Will our writing last? Will it stay in print after we're gone? In their grumbling about how publishing houses didn't understand or promote them, the Western writer once bet the Southwestern writer ten dollars that his next book, *Dancers in the Scalp House,* would sell fewer copies than *The Monkey Wrench*

Gang. Eastlake won the bet. What it came down to, the two assured each other, was that in their writing about Western America, they had "fought the good fight."

Eastlake comes to mind best whenever I'm in Bisbee and walk down Main Street. All I have to do is glance over at Café Roka, an upscale restaurant in a building where the Tavern—a good, working-class bar—used to be. You could look through the front door of The Tavern and see light streaming in through the back. Many mornings, after Eastlake had dropped his companion Marilyn off at work, he would stop by and sit alone at the bar, nursing a schooner of beer. Backlit against the clear mountain sun, cowboy hat in place, his profile soothed passersby. He was "erect and spare," as he described a character in *Castle Keep,* "like an old polished sword, but unbending, fragile and hard."

~

Eastlake's West had colors, rutted roads, and sparse dialogue. Abbey's land was tactile, almost prickly; his fiction was motivational. Their writing had little in common, yet they wrote with an affectionate respect for the land and those who contend with it. Abbey's contribution to the American lexicon may well be the verb "to monkey wrench." The phenomenon—clandestine sabotage in the name of environmental preservation—reached an invigorating plateau in the early Reagan years, when the soft-cover edition of *The Monkey Wrench Gang* was circulating hip pocket to backpack, briefcase to purse. To many, *The Monkey*

Wrench Gang was both old and new testament. One day in 1983, members of Earth First!—a defiantly radical and joyfully anarchic environmental group—straggled into the Lake Powell area from the Lone Rock campgrounds just across the state line in Utah. Interior Secretary James Watts had accepted an invitation to celebrate the 20th anniversary of tourist-oriented Lake Powell, a body of water that fills the sandstone Glen Canyon and attracts more than two million tourists a year. Earth First!ers, who looked like they had spent the previous six months in the wilderness and enjoyed every minute of it, had come for a glimpse of the evil incarnate that was James Watt. He did not disappoint them.

Yet James Watt's enemies always underestimated him. When he addressed an overflow luncheon of corporate well-wishers and tourism honchos at a lodge owned by the Del Webb Corporation that day, he spoke with symmetry: When his left arm rose outward to the sky, so did his right, giving the impression of a minister in mid-benediction. He turned 45 degrees to the left, then 45 to the right. His body expanded and contracted. He followed gratuitous insults to his detractors and the press with heaping praise for his own accomplishments. His ten fingers touched lightly, as if holding a softball. Even his incisors were uniform. A mock-up of Rainbow Bridge, the popular 290-foot-high symmetrical sandstone formation at Lake Powell, formed a halo behind his head.

Watt's philosophy of federal land use? Simple: Any land under his control was wasted unless it produced revenue, whether from mineral rights, grazing fees, or tourism. Land that remains pristine and undeveloped might as well be fallow fields; turn it over to private enterprise, he insisted. And an unalloyed example of Watt's philosophy? Right there at Lake Powell, where "more people have rafted since the dam was built than rafted it from the day of Adam"—where, he announced, there should be further development of tourist facilities and where "there will never be a ban on motorized rafting on the Colorado River as long as I hold office. If you're going to be a steward you've got to invest in the land." His audience slurped it up. But while he spoke, a small plane was gassing up at a nearby airfield. Soon it would fly overhead, trailing an Earth First! banner reading "FREE THE COLORADO!"

Earth First! defined environmental approaches as either deep or shallow ecology. The latter involved compromises, trade-offs, and planned development of wilderness areas; its practitioners ranged widely, from Morris and Stewart Udall to James Watt, from the Sierra Club to the Del Webb Corporation. Deep ecology rejected this approach, arguing that every trade-off and compromise, no matter how well-intentioned, forever reduced the Earth. Privately, some were "two-hatters," working on acceptable Sierra Club goals while simultaneously pursuing absolutist objectives. "Never again," said purist Earth First!ers of projects such as the Glen Canyon Dam. They were the Jewish Defense League of the environmental movement.

To celebrate Lake Powell's 20th birthday, Watt and the other guests boarded a paddleboat for a short ceremonial ride. At the same time, Earth First! rented a houseboat from a Del Webb fleet and motored within sight of the VIP paddleboat. From my vantage point on the top deck of the latter, I could see the demonstrators on the former, but their anti-Watt chants were unintelligible. A Paradise Valley matron to my side noticed that I was peering out at the friendly rabble. "Earthworms," she said with a harrumph, "that's what they are." She considered that an insult. Others on the VIP float regarded Earth First! more with condescension than contempt, looking on them as they might view trained seals at the San Diego zoo.

A few minutes later the transmission on our vessel malfunctioned and it refused to budge. We were up Lake Powell without a paddleboat; this wasn't the *Titanic,* but it was a potential public-relations disaster. Del Webb publicists, skilled in damage control, immediately sprang into action: They poured glass after glass of champagne for the VIPs until the problem was solved. Arizona Governor Bruce Babbitt took part in the public ceremonies, then the future Interior Secretary privately praised Abbey. I wandered over to a fellow wearing a white cowboy hat and a dark bola tie. It was Interior Secretary James Watt. He told me that a few weeks earlier he had been touring national parks in Alaska, and a ranger asked if he could borrow his glasses. Watt, a bit puzzled, handed them over, he related, and the ranger put them on for a few silent seconds, then handed them back. "Thank you, Mr. Secretary. I just wanted a chance to see how you saw the world."

I asked: "Mr. Secretary, are you familiar with *The Monkey Wrench Gang?*"

"Is that the book about eco— eco— eco—" The cabinet member stammered like a stuck record, his mouth powerless to utter the word in full.

"Ecotage?" I suggested.

"Yes, that's it. No, I'm not really familiar with it."

"It's set in this area."

"Really? In Navajoland?"

"No. Here at Lake Powell. At the dam."

"Well!"

A reporter from the *Lake Powell Chronicle* joined us. "It's a novel. A very funny book about blowing up the dam. A fantasy."

"No. Obviously I've not read it."

"I'll get you a copy," the local journalist offered.

"I never promise to read anything," Watt replied.

Around the Earth First! campfire that night, a gaggle of good-natured environmental ruffians laughed at how silly they themselves had looked, how the odds were so stacked against them as to be incalculable, how off-key were the ditties they had sung from their "Li'l Green Song Book." I bought a REDNECKS FOR WILDERNESS T-shirt from them for ten dollars. They spoke of a fall propaganda tour taking their songs, skits, and message through Midwest and East Coast campuses. They talked of Ludlow, Bisbee, Butte, Silver City, and other Western towns where militant miners had stood up to recalcitrant companies. They warbled rock-and-roll tunes by such environmentalists as Bo Diddley, Ritchie Valens, and the Isley Brothers. They made up songs featuring Watt, Reagan, and Glen Canyon, though they were hard-pressed to find a rhyme for Ruck-elshaus. As they tossed the last log on their campfire, the self-anointed Earth First! Tabernacle Choir howled a particularly rousing "Up Against the Wall, Redneck Mother." The Colorado River continued to flow into Lake Powell with a mind of its own, only to emerge lobotomized at the far end.

∼

Ed Abbey was a fortunate novelist. While he was writing *The Monkey Wrench Gang* in the early 1970s, he must have taken encouragement and inspiration from events around the country. A Vermont man calling himself Lobo sawed down billboards on highways throughout New England and as far south as the Key Bridge connecting Virginia to Washington, D.C. "The Fox" of Kane County, Illinois, dumped sludge and dead fish at a U.S. Steel executive's office, so enraged was he at that company's befouling of the air and water. A man in Montague, Massachusetts, toppled a 500-foot tower to be used in nuclear power-plant construction. Elsewhere in New England, 30 high school students were caught with axes that would have been perfect for chopping down billboards, but the police lacked evidence and had to let them go.

Along Route 93 in Idaho's Sun Valley, billboards fell as fast as they could be replaced. Likewise on Highway 50 near Virginia City, Nevada. College students in Prescott, Arizona, acknowledged using saws and axes on billboards lining Highway 89 north of town. These were just some of the episodes that earned one-paragraph wire stories around the country. Never underestimate the power of the Associated Press to spread seditious acts.

I trace my own antipathy toward unsightly billboards to the mid-1950s, when I was in grade school. My father, a Washington, D.C., lawyer, worked for an attorney whose clients included the

Outdoor Advertising Council—a gussied-up euphemism for the billboard lobby. Our family often drove south through the Blue Ridge Mountains, where billboards were already an eyesore.

"Dad," I said in exasperation during one trip, "how can you represent the billboard industry?"

He looked at me with mock seriousness. "Combats highway hypnosis."

While all the billboarding was going on throughout the country, a gang of four in Tucson, Arizona, enjoyed a two-year run. Their target was real estate developments, and their aim was to slow down housing construction that leapfrogged through the valley and up the mountainsides. They had neither political theory nor context and saw neither historical precedent nor overarching principles. They sought no greater goal than acting as flame retardant to the firestorm of development burning the desert. The initial group had been friends at Canyon Del Oro High School, and most went on to the University of Arizona. They called themselves the Eco-Raiders, and they did their homework.

The Eco-Raiders denounced developers who chopped down cactus willy-nilly on the periphery of town, who built in floodplains, and, as in that old cliché, raped the land. They fought home builders with sabotage. They targeted suburban growth that debilitated the delicate balance plants needed to flourish and animals required to propagate. Their moonlight forays became the desert's rape-crisis center. At the time neither Tucson nor Pima County had a comprehensive growth plan. The Eco-Raiders became the anti-growth plan.

To decelerate housing development meant attacking it at the point of sale. The Eco-Raiders initially went after new-home advertising on billboards, then escalated to assaulting model homes and earth-moving equipment. Almost always they left a note explaining their exploits. Their calling card was a big spray-painted STOP URBAN SPRAWL left at their attack sites, followed by their name. They skipped construction sites that abided by their four-point program: cluster housing, natural plant-life preservation, open spaces for playgrounds, and homes built outside floodplains.

The Eco-Raiders usually went out around ten at night in an anonymous pickup. Three of them, wearing bandannas to shield their identities and gloves to keep their fingerprints to themselves, would hop out with a two-man saw and spray paint. They'd saw down a land-promoter's billboard in the desert, usually one advertising a new development. If there was a convenient flat surface nearby, they'd leave their calling card. The driver would swing by a designated pickup point once every 20 minutes. The raids took place frequently, at least a couple of times a week.

The Eco-Raiders enjoyed warm press relations; whenever they left a note explaining their attitude, the town's dailies would dutifully report it. They wrote local officials in block printing on lined paper:

> BEING APPALLED BY THE UNCHECKED SPREAD
> OF URBAN SPRAWL, WE ARE PROMPTED TO
> CONTACT YOU AGAIN AND REQUEST THAT YOU
> TAKE ACTION. PLEASE—STOP PROTECTING

DEVELOPERS WHO ARE DESTROYING THE EARTH FOR PROFIT. IT IS TIME TO OFFER TAX INCENTIVES OR DEMAND BY LAW THAT BETTER USE BE MADE OF THE LAND... FOR THE PAST SEVERAL WEEKS WE HAVE DESTROYED AN AVERAGE OF AT LEAST ONE REALTOR OR LAND DEVELOPMENT SIGN A DAY. WITH THE HELP OF MORE CONCERNED CITIZENS WE SHALL RAISE THAT TO TWO A DAY. STOP URBAN SPRAWL BEFORE IT'S TOO LATE!!!

—ECO-RAIDERS

Not only did they have a commendable cause, they were polite and familiar with the law—and they knew how to use the apostrophe.

Initially, home builders and sellers were befuddled. No one had ever publicly challenged them; rezoning hearings had always been pro forma. Suddenly they became defensive, unsure how to counteract such bold and multipronged attacks. After the Eco-Raiders escalated to smashing windows on model homes, pouring sand down fuel tanks of earth-moving equipment, and ripping the wires out of homes under construction, the housing industry got really pissed. Their free handout to prospective home buyers addressed the issue head-on: "These ecology-minded bands wear black robes and mumble chants while they do their 'good deeds' to save society from itself." The head of the Home Builders Association reduced their position to an orthographic formula. "They want N-O growth, and we want K-N-O-W growth. That's the difference."

The Eco-Raiders became minor folk heroes. People talked about them at cocktail parties and keggers, at water coolers and in barrooms. If the public's attitude was not 100 percent supportive, at least it brought attention to the subject. Copycat groups sprang up and used the same name. The war against Vietnam was in full throttle, and the growing Watergate scandal further diluted respect for government. Most agreed with the Eco-Raiders' objectives but wavered on their technique. (One fellow I met told me he approved of their methods but not their goals.) The Eco-Raiders posed the philosophical question, What is the sound of one billboard falling?

Myself, I rather admired their spunk and hoped to ride with them one night. I placed a classified ad in the alternative weekly *New Times* asking the Eco-Raiders to get in touch. Using techniques gleaned from B movies, I arranged for callers to the newspaper to be given the number of a phone booth where a friend would refer them to me at yet another phone booth— somewhat like a three-corner billiard shot. Most callers thought I was recruiting, not seeking. Among them was a female detective whose ploy was pitifully obvious. In my notes I scribbled, "und-covr—cn't they d/bettr thn ths?"

Deciphering who among the callers was the real McCoy was surprisingly simple, and in short order the Eco-Raiders trusted me enough to invite me along for a raid. If you have confidence in me, I told them, you'll have to trust my photographer too; they did. On the appointed night they sent us to a gas station, whose pay phone Yellow Pages hid our instructions—a very neatly drawn map directing us to what was then the northeastern edge of the city. At a specific point we were to make a U-turn and park by a 45-mph sign near a power substation. "Be careful," an arrowed note on the map cautioned, "there is an identical sign *here.*" We were to turn off our engine and roll down the right front window. We were given an "Out of Gas" sign to put on my car.

We parked at the wrong sign, my photographer and I, and almost missed the rendezvous. After 25 minutes, two members of a band of Eco-Raiders came hiking up to us, somewhat short of breath and not at all pleased with our mistake. We all slithered out of sight into an area where homes were under construction.

We had a lovely saguaro's-eye view of the city's twinkling lights, a view that would attract any home buyer. The group's spokesman, whom I guessed to be five-ten and 165 pounds, wore a knit hat, a stocking over his face, an army-surplus jacket, black gloves, and heavy boots. We sat as he answered my interview questions on tape for 20 minutes. Suddenly the group rose as one and went over to a previously stacked pile of rocks. They each took a softball-size rock and heaved them at the windows of two half-built homes. The windows were thick and the rocks weren't entirely effective, so the gang pulled a couple of crowbars from their clothing and finished the glass off with a few well-aimed whacks. The spokesman slipped inside the house and sprayed STOP URBAN SPRAWL—ECO-RAIDERS on the walls, then we filed back to the pickup point.

Frankly, I would have preferred your basic billboard chop-chop. Nonetheless, their vandalism was exhilarating, and I found myself hyperventilating. Mr. Spray Paint was as calm as a Tarahumara Indian running under a quarter moon. The Eco-Raiders bid us good night, and the photographer and I headed to a bar to sort out what we had just seen.

This sort of raid went on with continued impunity, and eventually the county sheriff's department took a hard look at the goings-on. In six weeks' time they fingered a likely suspect—who, with a promise of immunity, told all. As it happened, he had not accompanied us that night—the Eco-Raiders raided in shifts— but he sure knew enough to get the others arrested.

The main Eco-Raiders were sentenced to six months' county-jail time and fined less than a thousand dollars, each on misdemeanor vandalism charges. They also had to donate 300 hours' labor to the Pima County Environmental Health Department. The fellow behind the stocking mask that night—the one who had done most of the group's research and whose broadsides articulated their intents—was John Walker. A few years later, I bumped into John while shopping. He was making a living drawing nicely rendered line sketches of Southwest characters and selling them on the shopping-mall circuit. We reminisced about the Eco-Raiders, and he gave me a framed sketch of two Indians relaxing.

The other day I took out the map to the raid site for the first time in years and drove up to the construction spot in the foothills of the Santa Catalina Mountains where I'd met up with John and his buddies. It is now a gated community called Casa Sunrise. I tried to imagine what the land would look like if the Eco-Raiders had had their way.

CHAPTER 3

JACK RUBY'S KITCHEN SINK

Aweekend auction I attended in central Texas in 1972 vexed me for a long time. Was it commerce? History? Political science? Finally it struck me: It was art. The Athens Transfer and Storage Company warehouse was the gallery, the items on display were the pieces of art, and we bidders were the unwitting actors in an elaborate one-act play.

I realized it was art years later when Jacqueline Kennedy's personal effects were auctioned off at a $34.5 million Sotheby's festival of excess. Myriad explanations were given, but most bidders there said they simply wanted "a piece of history." That's what the New York and Texas events had in common. But I had no context for that in the early 1970s; we were simply pioneers in the Kennedy memorabilia business, unaware of the precedent—artistic or otherwise—we were setting.

Rewind to television's first live murder: sleazy nightclub owner Jack Ruby killing Kennedy assassination-suspect Lee Harvey Oswald in the basement of the Dallas City Hall, November 24, 1963. "You all know me," Ruby proclaimed to posterity. "I'm Jack Ruby."

And so he was. Ruby was seized, of course, and lived out his remaining four years in jail. His tawdry Carousel Club closed down in short order, and the building's owner eventually mothballed all the club's fixtures in Athens, 75 miles southeast of Dallas. After a few years Ruby's former landlord got tired of paying monthly storage fees and arranged to turn everything over to Johnny Stiles, the Athens warehouse owner. In due time Stiles, then about 40, figured the Ruby collection was taking up too much space. He took on a couple of investors and announced to the world that he would be auctioning off all the fixtures from Jack Ruby's Carousel Club. That auction, less than nine years after President Kennedy was killed, launched the whole JFK memorabilia industry, a phenomenon that climaxed 24 years later at Sotheby's.

At the time of the Athens event, Jacqueline Kennedy was married to Aristotle Onassis, Dallas had recently won Super Bowl VI, and Marlon Brando had just refused his Oscar for *The Godfather*. We were earlobe deep in Vietnam, and Watergate meant nothing more than a fancy Foggy Bottom address.

Every art auction has its pièce de résistance to attract connoisseurs. At Athens, the piece no one could resist was Ruby's 800-pound safe, said to have not been opened since Carousel Club days. In the weeks leading up to the auction, guessing the safe's contents was common among the good people of Athens. A map of Dealey Plaza? An envelope stuffed with money? A diagram of the Dallas City Hall basement? Marching orders from the mafia? Evidently the bad people of Athens were thinking along the same lines. The night before the auction, thieves pried open the Faulk

Street warehouse door and stole the safe. The still-unsolved theft was a great contribution to conspiracy lore, but not much help to Johnny Stiles and his auction.

I remember this much: When I traveled over to the auction in Athens, Texas, gas cost 21.9¢ a gallon and the town was "the black-eyed pea capital of the world." A chamber of commerce brochure said the world's first hamburger was cooked there. The artifacts to be auctioned constituted an odd lot, and I must say we bidders did likewise: café owners looking for fixtures, historians looking for history, nearby ranching and farm families dropping in during Saturday shopping, a sprinkling of assassination buffs, as well as the macabre and the just plain curious. Many in the crowd looked like they had recently spotted UFOs. A couple of bidders flew their private jets to the local airport.

Among the goods: a brass chandelier, clothes racks, a stove, metal closets, chairs, a dish rack, kitchen utensils, an ice-cream freezer, and the object of my desire, Jack Ruby's kitchen sink.

The safe had been the big draw, but as we bidder-actors milled around looking over the goods before the auction, we consoled ourselves that the leftovers were worthwhile, too. The first item on the block was a Carousel Club barstool. A short fellow in a small cowboy hat walked away with it for $26. Jack Ruby's lime squeezer—it once squeezed Jack Ruby's limes—fetched $7. A busted cash register extracted $31. Broken corks, rusty silverware, furniture in need of repair—they all brought under $25. When some napkin holders went on the block, I stepped out to the local Dairy Queen. On my return, I was chagrined to learn that while

I was gone the sink had gone, too. It brought in $12. A stage-light shell, the Club's bathroom scale, and some knickknacks together garnered less than $20. The Carousel sign raised a hubbub, then went for a disappointing $6.

The auctioneer, a seasoned pro, brought up Ruby's name only when enthusiasm waned, but for the most part he kept the JFK assassination out of his patter. The day's highest bid of $200 bought a metallic engraving of a horse, mounted on wood. We were a hundred strong at our peak, and the horse engraving was the one electric moment. Unbeknownst to most bidders, Stiles's two silent partners in the auction stood to the rear, jacking up the price on sale items. As it turns out, they were lousy shills. Their bid on Jack Ruby's 400 folding chairs was never topped, and they were stuck essentially paying themselves for the near-useless items. They were the only two people present who lost money on the auction.

I realized that Johnny Stiles was fast running out of items, and if I wanted anything at all, I had best bid—pronto. I raised one finger as I glanced at the auctioneer with a silent half-nod. He returned the nod, and when none of the 50 or so others remaining topped my bid, Jack Ruby's can opener was mine for one dollar. I had doubled the previous offer. I kicked myself for stepping out while the kitchen sink went up for bids, but I took solace in my day's booty. Perhaps I thought it would open the whole can of worms.

∾

Impulsively ghoulish reactions to sorrowful tragedy certainly did not start with Kennedy assassination artifacts. When Louis XVI was decapitated in 1793, people smeared his blood on their foreheads for good luck. A young lad is said to have created a souvenir by dipping a white handkerchief in Louis's fresh blood. Compared to that, a rusty can opener nine years after the fact meant nothing.

Far more ghastly was another auction I attended the year following my trip to Athens, Texas. This auction, held under a circus tent in a Scottsdale hotel parking lot, drew some 1,500 spectators. The draw: two cars documented to have been in Adolf Hitler's private fleet. The auction drew people who wanted to take home a piece of *der Führer.*

Bidding started slowly, then accelerated. The auctioneer working for Tom Barrett, owner of both Hitler cars for sale that day, became visibly excited when the bidding topped $100,000. A New Jersey couple, exhibitors on the state-fair and shopping-mall circuit, wanted to buy one of Hitler's five-ton Mercedes-Benzes to take on tour. Their enormous Belgian draft horse was dying of cancer and they needed a new attraction. "This car has the potential to pay for itself!" the auctioneer shouted. Barrett, sitting in the driver's seat, pushed a button under the dashboard that set off a piercing siren; the audience erupted with a roar of support. Much of it, I felt disconsolately certain, was for the car's symbolic value.

The auctioneer must have sensed that things were going too far. "This car has got its place in history," he reminded the bidders. "Adolf Hitler was probably the worst criminal that ever lived, and there is no one that ever wants to say a good word for him. But there's a lot of people," he went on, "when they look at this vehicle it brings back memories of the way not to be." More applause followed his monologue, heightened by another horn blast.

The bidding on Hitler's Mercedes rose yet again when the owner of a Lancaster, Pennsylvania, amusement park entered the fray. "When you're spending that kind of money," the auctioneer said, "another five or ten thousand dollars doesn't make any difference." Barrett's wife stepped into the backseat, her fur coat pressed snug up against the Nazi insignia draped over the rear. Their young son took the jump seat. The bidding soon became a battle between the New Jersey shopping-mall exhibitors and the Pennsylvania amusement-park owner—Easterners both, who had come West seeking our most vile ornaments. The man from Pennsylvania bought Adolf Hitler's car for $153,000.

By the time Tom Barrett, whose Hitler cars formed part of his antique car collection, drove the second one into the Scottsdale circus tent, a third of the crowd had drifted away. The final bid of $93,000 came from a wiry Alabaman who hoped to take the car on a tour of state fairs.

Yet a third Hitler car was said to reside in Arizona, this one parked at an Interstate 10 tourist trap called "The Thing?" Imagine your own revulsion on moving to a new part of the country and passing roadside billboards urging you to SEE HITLER'S ROLLS ROYCE.

The Hitler car auction in Scottsdale put my desire for Jack Ruby's kitchen sink in perspective. Still, to call a slightly corroded can opener or a newly polished antique car a piece of history invites consideration of just what anoints an object as historical. Is it the item's intrinsic worth, who put it to use, or the use it was put to? The auction in Scottsdale, loathsome and reprehensible, sat on the lowest rung of show business. The ones at Athens and Sotheby's, each in its own way, redefined history—and with it the notion of value and the value of notions.

For years I carefully stowed my prize can opener deep in a file drawer at home, wrapped in a piece of chamois. On rare occasions when I thought a visitor would appreciate its unique qualities, I would take it out with impish pride and hold it up as a totem of American history. I mentioned the can opener in a nonfiction book on the broader subject of the ceaseless captivation that the Dallas assassination has held, but it wasn't until much later that I saw it immortalized in fiction, when David Quammen, in his spy thriller *The Soul of Victor Tronko,* wrote of a retired editor who had bought Jack Ruby's can opener at an auction "Not for any evidentiary value, God knows, but just as a ghoulish sort of souvenir. A rusty can opener. He carried it wrapped in a piece of chamois."

These days I store my prize objet d'art, still wrapped in chamois, in a Bank of America safe-deposit box. Not for any evidentiary value, God knows, but as a self-conscious reminder of its curious significance. The Texans who joined me on that long-ago afternoon were more confident. "I bet that's going to be worth a thousand dollars some day," said a man in a big straw hat to his bald-headed neighbor as he loaded a tarnished dish rack into his pickup after the auction.

"Yup. That's what I'm counting on."

"I got these for my young'uns," said Straw Hat, pointing to some small old tables at his side, "to give my kids a little something from their Dad."

This was the Southwest at its modern most: mercantile, enigmatic, and inappropriately hopeful.

Indeed, if bidders at Sotheby's Kennedy sale preened their upper-class pretensions, the Jack Ruby auction drew working-class desire. Buyers at both wanted a bankable piece of history. As for the Athens investors, they should have kept their Carousel Club loot until the market heated up. Imagine what they could get today for Jack Ruby's kitchen sink.

~

Art developed in the Southwest has appreciated in value considerably in the last few decades. When you think of quality art from this region, a Georgia O'Keeffe flower petal may come to mind. Or R. C. Gorman's lush stylized Indian lithographs. Or Ansel Adams's famous photograph "Moon Over Interstate 25." Yet for sheer quantity, borderland art beats them all. The borderland acts as its trampoline; we import it by the semi-full from just over the line in Mexico and ship it to points throughout the States and Canada. I speak, of course, of black velvet paintings—the ultimate NAFTA art form.

To see acrylic black velvet at swap meets and flea markets is to appreciate art *en su jus.* Elvis Presley. Dogs playing poker. Nudes with arched backs. Bullfights. UFOs. Those are the perennials. Other subjects stay in fashion for a while, then fade: a white-suited John Travolta. Madonna. John Lennon. Michael Jackson. To learn who will be on next week's black velvet, look at this week's *People.*

The art of velvet also infiltrates America in more devious ways. "Sylvia," the cartoon creation of Nicole Hollander, once dreamed she was the high bidder at a Christie's auction for a black-velvet Dan Quayle. Julian Schnabel has dabbled on black velvet, filling enormous canvases with explosive expressionism. In an explanation that would baffle most velvet artists, an art professor once rationalized the New York art world's involvement with black velvet for me: "The East Village art scene of the 1980s rebelled against the SoHo and uptown art scene by creating off-the-wall art. The use of velvet is a way of rebelling against high art." In San Francisco, Paul Mavrides blurs the distinction between high and popular art, as well as low, dada, and nada. A critically acclaimed artist, Mavrides's weirder pieces include a black-velvet Mao Tse-tung with doleful Keene eyes, Jackie Kennedy climbing out of the back of the limo in Dealey Plaza, the *Challenger* explosion, the aftermath of Jim Jones's Kool-Aid party, Oliver North, AIDS devouring a victim, and a glass crack pipe. "I choose these horrifying subjects for velvet because they're so repugnant. You're attracted to the repulsion. Velvet simply magnifies the push-pull quality."

Is it art? Is it tacky? A resounding and prideful yes to both. Black velvet has the ability to deprecate its subject while magnifying itself. The medium overwhelms the message. To call paintings on black velvet unimaginative would be redundant. It is rather like an elderly uncle in the corner whose constant burps and farts embarrass everyone but him.

There is a terrific scene in the 1979 movie *The In-Laws* in which CIA agent Peter Falk tours the palace of a Central American dictator. Black velvet paintings hang on every wall. "General," Falk says, deadpan, "your art collection never fails to take my breath away." The clueless dictator replies, pointing to a tiger on black velvet for which he paid $25,000, "Note the plasticity. The use of perspective."

Such plasticity and perspective go back almost half a century. In 1955, a young Mexican artist, Jaime Dante Cortés, was asked to paint a Virgin of Guadalupe on the skirt of a Monterrey dancer about to embark on a tour of the United States. The skirt was made of black velvet, a texture Dante found to his liking for its light and shadows, its economy, and its ease of preparation. According to *Texas Monthly,* the first black-velvet painting on record then traveled north from Mexico. As for Dante, he bought bolts of black *terciopelo* and began cranking out bullfights and landscapes, works that quickly found a receptive market in the States.

That's one version of how it began. But you can no more accurately pinpoint the birth of painting on black velvet than you can the first chimichanga or the first Our Lady of Guadalupe mural. There are wholesalers in Juárez and distributors in El Paso who are convinced the art form came from their twin cities; likewise in Ambos Nogales and Los Dos Laredos. And proponents of Edgar Leeteg, an American artist who lived in Tahiti, insist that Leeteg's pre-World War II velvet art set a precedent. Black velvet art confirms the theory of independent but simultaneous evolution.

A fellow border rat once assured me that black-velvet art gets better as you head west. According to this theory, Tijuana makes the best in the land. I well recall once slipping down to Baja California from San Diego in search of the king of black velvet. Curio shop owners on Tijuana's Avenida Revolución each boasted that they had the best and least expensive black-velvet art, paintings so valueless they casually leaned them against their storefronts in direct sunlight. Most acknowledged that they bought from the same man, a fellow whose bodega, a few blocks south, was stacked floor to ceiling with exquisitely tasteless paintings. His best seller that week was a glow-in-the-dark work of the Golden Gate Bridge stretching from San Francisco to the moon.

The wholesaler was agreeable and talkative, and when I asked about the next level up, he escorted me on foot to a nearby colonia. "Almost all of us buy from one of three factories," he told me during the 20-minute stroll to the neighborhood. "They set the price. We double theirs, and the merchants double ours."

The wholesaler introduced me to a well-dressed man at the door of a double-wide garage in a residential district. "Come in, won't you please?" the man said with the unctuous charm of a border-town hustler. Inside I was confronted by an astonishing spectacle: a dozen young men all sitting in a row at a counter, each intently painting an acrylic Last Supper on black velvet. The fellow nearest me was just starting to set the table. The light-skinned man next to him was working on the ceiling. Jesus and his disciples were the focus of the teenager to his right. A youngster walked around the workplace with large buckets of paint so each artist could replenish his supply without interrupting his oeuvre. Out back another youth unspooled meter after meter of velvet, then cut it with enormous scissors while his compañero stretched it onto wood in three consumer-friendly sizes. It was an extraordinary assembly line—a black-velvet factory.

My host headed the local velvet-artists union, but he worked for the distributors, not the artists. Most of his workers put in 12-hour shifts and received less than minimum wage. Each had a quota of 40 paintings a day. "These muchachos," the velvet *macher* said with a sweep of his hand, "they come from the interior with the intention of crossing. They are talented but they are hungry. After they've worked here a few weeks, they try to go north. Some come back and settle in. I have a few who've been with me a couple of years." Turnover was indeed very high for these artists without portfolio, but the notion that a velvet-art sweatshop slows down northbound traffic could only be good news for the Immigration and Naturalization Service. Increased demand for black-velvet art would mean more such factories. To solve America's insoluble immigration dilemma, I suggest we buy more Last Suppers, more Elvises, and more UFOs on black velvet.

≈

Black-velvet specialists are happy to paint custom jobs. They usually work overnight from images clipped from magazines. If you supply them with a photograph, your one-of-a-kind black-velvet portrait will be ready the next day. I considered commissioning a painting of Jack Ruby's kitchen sink on black velvet, but thought that might be taking bad art too far. Still, black velvet art has come a long way from the Virgin of Guadalupe. But the Virgin of Guadalupe has come a long way herself. She's been on black velvet, tortillas, and in recent decades, bola ties.

Not too long ago I paid ten dollars for a very nice bola featuring the Virgin of Guadalupe surrounded by a harp and a saxophone. Bola ties have gone from hokey Western wear to kitschy high-fashion accessories. They continue to spread, from Southwestern retired men's clubs to trendy East Village nightclubs; their styles vary from Native American to new wave and punk. Clasp anything you want to a string, and you have your own individualized bola tie.

Like velvet art, the bola tie has its own firmly enshrined mythology. One day in the late 1940s when Vic Cedarstaff was out riding near Wickenburg, Arizona, a gust of wind lifted his cowboy hat off his head; it hit the ground and the leather, silver-tipped band slipped off the hat. "He retrieved both and hastily slipped the hatband around his neck," wrote Bill Kramer in *Bola Tie: New Symbol of the West.* "One of his companions noticed it and said, 'Nice tie you've got there, Vic.'"

A myth created, a fashion born.

Cedarstaff, also a silversmith and leatherworker, started making string ties of braided cord with a silver slide and, dangling from the tips, silver balls. He called them "piggin' neckties" because they resembled the piggin' string cowboys used to hog-tie calves. Fortunately the name didn't stick, and when a friend mentioned that the ties resembled the Argentine boleadora—a contraption with three braids weighted with stones used to catch cattle—Cedarstaff appropriated its nickname for his own creation. This all happened far enough back that historical verification would be fruitless, and perhaps pointless.

The overriding image of bola ties is that they're corny and dorky, worn by humorless white men who seldom commit taste or fashion. For the most part that image holds true. The bola tie is cousin to black-velvet art, and like its cousin, occasionally slips out of character to surprise and amaze. The classic bola is made of tightly braided string or plastic cord around the neck joined by turquoise or some other rock mounted on a slide. But new-wave designers have expanded the boilerplate bola to include computer chips, spiffy jewelry, and creative motifs. One I saw exhibited features a sterling-silver baseball; another, a miniature dinner of two tacos, rice, and beans. Yet another sported a tuxedoed coyote howling at the naked moon. A Crested Butte, Colorado, man crafted a bola showing a chimpanzee working its way up the evolutionary ladder to a rancher; it's called "Darwin's Cowboy." In Phoenix, the Heard Museum collection includes classics from Zuni, Hopi, and Navajoland; in Santa Fe, where high-end bolas sell for thousands of dollars, the bola boom has been good to artists. Clearly, the bola tie has been blown about on the shifting sands of Southwestern chic.

Bola ties have their practical advantages: They're ambisexual; you can wear them with a T-shirt, jeans, a business suit, or—as the late

Arizona Republican senator Barry Goldwater often did—with a tuxedo at black-tie affairs; you can put them on at a stop sign or at the front door. If salad dressing spills on yours, you can clean it off with a moist towelette, no dry-cleaning necessary. They don't need loosening and they don't constrict your neck; one size fits all. The nicest thing about wearing bola ties is that they will never go out of fashion because they never came into it.

The biggest change in Bolandia during the last generation is that women now design, buy, and wear them. This has made for an entirely brighter, more lively marketplace, bringing the renegade bola perilously close to respectability. This agreeable development suits everyone except the Bola Tie Society of Arizona, founded in 1966 by Bill Close, a Phoenix television-news personality who retired in 1990. Close and his buddies lobbied the state government hard—not for education funds, indigent health care, or wilderness preservation, but to make the bola tie the state's official neckwear. In 1971 they were triumphant, and Arizona, certainly one of the few states with such a designation, named Vic Cedarstaff's creation the "state neckwear." It replaced the rope.

The Bola Tie Society, an all-male organization, meets monthly at a second-rate Phoenix restaurant to laugh at off-color jokes told by president-for-life Bill Close. They invited me to one meeting, and to satisfy their dress code I chose a bola with a smartly hand-tinted photo of a saguaro cactus framed inside a slide, mounted on a standard plastic string. As lunch was served, each member stood in turn to address the day's topic: "My very first bola tie." Close, who moved to Arizona in 1946, had his own theory on the bola's popularity. "Everybody here is from someplace else. Wearing a bola helps fortify a new identity."

The fellow to my left wore one with a two-ounce gold Zuni eagle in flight, its jaws clutching a fish made of ivory. Next to him was a tie adorned with 15 diamonds surrounding an 18-carat gold phoenix with a sapphire in its eye. The bola on the diner to my right had a metal thunderbird wearing a turquoise headdress. It was so big he could have umpired home plate and used his bola as a chest protector. Close himself wore the club bola, a sterling-silver laughing saguaro flexing its arms.

"You'll notice there're no women here," Close said. "It's because we like to tell raunchy jokes." A few months earlier a woman jewelry designer who was game for the experience asked to join. She presented her credentials to polite silence and left, after which her application was voted down 38-0. "We're just a bunch of conservative old farts," the president-for-life told me afterward. "It's a men's club. She was a women's libber."

On my way out the door a retiree from Minnesota pulled me aside. "Velcro." He had been quiet throughout the meeting, and now wanted to teach me an important lesson. "Velcro," he repeated, "for safety, especially children's. You should connect your bola at the back with Velcro instead of any other material"—he showed me his tie—"that way if anyone wants to strangle you with your bola, it'll come apart rather than twist around your neck." I thanked the man from Minnesota and dashed to the parking lot.

One would not think the bola controversial in the way that velvet art could be, but when the Arizona state capitol building hosted a bola-tie exhibit, it included a bronze figure of a sexually aroused naked man. Nervous officials placed a tiny loincloth over the man's organ, prompting court action by the bola maker. A judge ruled that authorities had no right to alter the tie, that the figure must appear in the altogether or be removed altogether. With six days to go in the show, authorities agreed to let the naked man stay—and to let him become naked again.

As for the Bola Tie Society, new members, who come from the ranks of the newly retired, are not sufficiently replacing the newly dead; and by the beginning of the 21st century, membership had dropped precipitously. "There just aren't too many people excited about wearing bola ties as there used to be," lamented still-president Bill Close. "We're becoming more civilized."

Every day Wolfe O'Maera, a veteran Bisbee jeweler and literary raconteur, wears the same corduroy jacket, a pistol, and one of two sweat-stained Stetsons. Over breakfast at the Turquoise Valley Country Club one morning, Wolfe and I conspired to design the world's ugliest bola tie. We discussed the tie's design and, more important, its philosophical contours. Two weeks later he called. "Tom," he said in his slow drawl, "I have made it. The world's ugliest bola. It will be my last one ever."

He presented it to me when we next got together. The string is really rope, quarter-inch hemp, hanging rope, the sort that preceded the bola as the state neckwear. The sliding adornment itself is a large piece of low-grade copper cut in the shape of

Arizona, with a simple stamped design around the edge. A chunk of fake turquoise dominates the state from the middle. Surrounding the faux mineral, Wolfe mounted sterling silver renditions of some of our most cherished stereotypes: a coyote howling at the moon, a saguaro cactus, a roadrunner, and a pick and shovel. A large brass star represents Bisbee in the state's southeastern corner.

But that's not all. Each end of the rope is tucked into a spent AK-47 cartridge, and to give it that certain *je ne sais quoi,* each cartridge is festooned with a dangling scorpion-under-plastic. It is exquisitely unsightly and certainly one-of-a-kind. In some states it would be a misdemeanor to carry such an implement. I have to surrender it when passing through airport metal detectors. Still, this incomparably unattractive fashion accessory is the ideal chunk of jewelry to wear when shopping for black-velvet paintings or to carry back East to give friends a taste of today's West.

～

Back East, of course, they have their own sense of today's West. For a while toward the end of the last century you could also find fake cactus, real cow skulls, wooden coyotes, and tumbleweed hangings in New York. Pretentious design shops, primarily in New York, unloaded their lacquered oriental jade and stocked up on rusty chain saw blades and crudely made Tarahumara instruments. Stores in SoHo sold southwesterly items for the skull 'n' cactus set that no one between Waco and Reno would look at twice. "New Yorkers," a New Yorker told me, "are willing to pay extraordinary prices for dried weeds." These people were called briefcase buckaroos.

Jim Griffith, the retired director of the University of Arizona's Southwest Folklore Center, received a call back then from the hanging-plants section of the *New York Times*. Among Manhattan interior decorators, dried cow skulls were all the rage that week, and the reporter wanted to know their significance. She had already interviewed Santa Fe arrivistes and Scottsdale trendies, and now she wanted an academic take on the phenomenon. Griffith replied that the skulls of dead cattle reminded local people of

Sculptor and friend lug a double-size desert icon down San Francisco Street, Santa Fe.

miserable droughts and to ascribe anything further to them was a disservice to the deceased. The up-tempo article that followed had no room for Jim Griffith's down-market honesty.

The manager of one store told me, "The New York metropolitan area and Long Island are so much more built up than Tucson and Phoenix. Here you're trapped; people like the mystique behind the desert. We do consulting. People call and say, 'How should I decorate my place to look Southwestern? What should I buy?'" The kitschy Southwestern shops turned a handsome profit supplying desert *tchotchkes* to art directors for background scenery in advertisements.

Once in New York I went to a store called Zona in SoHo, where uncomfortable wooden couches with silly designs painted on them were taken seriously, and overpriced cotton peasant blouses sold as fast as they could be produced. The incense alone could have induced allergies. Zona sold products, yes, but it delivered more on illusion and romance, and that accounted for its extraordinary popularity. With inscrutable wisdom the manager of an Upper West Side store told me, "The Southwest is more popular here than it is in the Southwest." Fortunately for all concerned, the Southwest scare seems to have blown over.

My effort to track down every whiff of faux Southwest led me to Best Arizona, a clothing store in Paris near Place de la République. The Palestinian owner had moved to France a few years earlier and hoped to earn enough money to return home and open a business.

"It's very fashionable to call things by American names here. They're very appealing. California, Texas, Montana. Personally, I like the image of the American West"—he wore pointy-toed Mexican cowboy boots—"but I chose the name for business reasons."

He had never been within 5,000 miles of the Grand Canyon, but he hoped to go to Los Angeles soon. "I want to find some scenes to put in the window of my store. Maybe a cowboy and a horse."

As I was leaving Best Arizona, the owner's wife walked in and he pointed at me. "Look! He's from Arizona!" She broke into a sudden grin and gave two thumbs up, as if the CBS cameras had found her in the stands at the NCAA playoffs. I was given a T-shirt solely on the basis of my zip code. Finally I visited Paradise City in Levallois, a northwest Paris suburb. They had a saguaro on their logo and sold phony Western-style clothes and cheap Mexican boots.

I related this disconcerting trend of Southwestiana to Mort Rosenblum, an Arizona journalist who lives on a houseboat moored to the right bank of the Seine. He nodded understanding and pointed to the boat's stern. There, Arizona's flag waited for a breeze to flap its copper star in the brisk Parisian night. Rosenblum put on his USS *Arizona* cap and fetched the manuscript of a book he was writing about his rediscovery of America during an extended home stay. "I've got a chapter on Tombstone and Tucson," he said, and proceeded to read a few pages aloud. His sadness and anger at his home state's willy-nilly overdevelopment rang clear and true, a latter-day echo of the Eco-Raiders' attitude, although too much sympathy was hard to muster for someone who began each day glimpsing the Eiffel Tower and rocked to sleep every night on the Seine. His last official tie to Arizona was a parcel of land he hoped to sell soon. "I used to have a saguaro at the office," he said, "but it died."

The culinary arts have done better than that saguaro in Paris. No dish represents the Southwest better than the chimichanga. It is both indigenous and, like the bola tie and velvet art, of indeterminate origin. Not long after settling in Arizona I went through a chimichanga period. My goal was to taste chimis in as many restaurants as possible. I was attracted to them for their name, of course, but also for their crunchiness and combination of textures: Outside the fried flour tortilla, you had melted cheese, sour cream, shredded lettuce, and salsa; inside, the all-important filling, anything from frijoles to beef, pork, chicken, chile, or whatever you wanted. Invariably it raised the philosophical question: Whence cometh the chimichanga? But one might as well ask about the sound of one hand clapping.

"There's no doubt in my mind how it came about," Carlotta Flores of El Charro in Tucson told me. "One day my Aunt Monica accidentally dropped a burrito into a vat of boiling lard. The next day it was on the menu."

El Charro's "disaster redeemed" story is countered by others who claim that Ronquillo's Bakery, also in Tucson, first served up chimichangas. Or Mi Ranchito, in Avondale, west of Phoenix. Definitely it was at Mi Nidito, replied the late Cora Borboa, who ran Cora's Café. "I can remember seeing chimichangas at the Yaqui Old Pascua Village in the mid-1950s," said folklorist Jim Griffith. A professor of Latin American Studies in Texas put the chimichanga in perspective: "It's hard to believe some Mexicans and Papagos in Arizona haven't been frying their burritos for generations. It simply took until the 1950s before they were served in restaurants."

Regardless of its ancestry, the chimichanga is a staple of Mexican restaurants throughout the Sonoran Desert. It is that most curious of foods—a Mexican dish neither born in Mexico nor widespread there. Start with a large flour tortilla so thin you can read the Gadsden Purchase through it, wrap it cylindrically around a filling, seal tightly, then deep-fry. Garnish *a su gusto.*

The chimichanga is the regional equivalent of creole gumbo or Florida stone crabs. It loads you up with 580 calories to burn off. (There is no such thing as a "chimichanga lite.") You know your chimichanga is authentic if an hour after eating it, you feel a log gently rolling around in your stomach. In many parts of the Southwest it is a first-class misdemeanor to be caught carrying a concealed chimichanga. The chimichanga is the gastronomical equivalent of war.

The chimichanga—the word loosely translates as "thingamabob"—has spawned its own culture and fanciers. In 1982, when Congressman Morris Udall had to choose which of two redrawn congressional districts to represent, he opted for the one with the best chimichangas. A high-end restaurant in Phoenix in his new district served a lobster chimichanga with leeks, goat cheese, and basil *beurre blanc.*

Since the late 1970s the chimichanga has crept onto menus throughout North America, as well as in Europe, Africa, and Asia. East Coasters have been known to ask friends flying in from Arizona to stop on the way to the airport and pick up authentic chimis to carry aboard with them. A transplant living in Australia once wrote me. "Please," he begged, "send me a chimichanga."

A Tucson journalist, having introduced Calvin Trillin to the chimichanga, fearfully predicted that the author would appraise the dish like this: "A cooler pad laced with strands of dried beef, rolled into a mailing tube and deep-fried." Nonetheless, for many years, whenever I'd return to Arizona after an extensive trip, I never really felt I was back home until I'd consumed a chimichanga. It is one of the great sensuous pleasures of the Southwest.

Rarely is the chimichanga ever ordered in the plural, although once after polishing off his very first chimi, a visiting Californian leaned back and smiled slowly. "That was great," he said, patting his stomach. "I think I'll have another." The name has often been bastardized, and almost always enjoyably so. At one place near Calexico, California, you can order a chivillanga. A New York acquaintance reports a chingachanga on one menu. But please, do not confuse the chimichanga with *chimurenga,* which means war of liberation in Shona, the principal Bantu language in Zimbabwe; nor with *chimba-chaca,* a crudely built cable suspension bridge in Ecuador; nor with *Chushingura,* Hiroshi Inagaki's samurai epic.

No matter what you call it, of course, you can always call it breakfast the next morning, when cold chimis meet their final fate.

SEARCHING FOR THE HEART OF "LA BAMBA"

If you choose your music carefully, you can concoct a soundtrack for your travels through the Southwest. Native American flute music by R. Carlos Nakai will harmonize your drive through the Four Corners region. In Mogollon Rim country, listen to Katie Lee sing original Western folk ballads. Passing through Tucson, crank up some hipster country music on a Dusty Chaps cassette. Listen to Joe Miguel and the Blood Brothers play chicken-scratch music as you drive by the Tohono O'odham and Pima reservations. (Don't forget native son Alice Cooper when you speed through Phoenix.) With Albuquerque's ethnic mix, you should listen to Native American band Red Earth play a reggae-punk-ska sound. A New Mexico friend recommends listening to Los Blues Ventures from Española for its small-village cantina sound, and farther north, the flamenco group Chuscales. The music of Los Lobos and Los Tigres del Norte, from outside the region, is likewise at home in the Southwest.

Still, it is possible that a single song can claim an entire region. "La Bamba"—a song that entered the United States when a clear-channel radio station in Mexico City broadcast it throughout the

Americas in the early 20th century—took root in the Southwest and West as campesino labor moved north from Mexico. Guitar by guitar, camp by camp, "La Bamba" spread. Entertainers picked it up, and jukeboxes carried the popular traditional versions. It is a song that goes well with main drags in big-city barrios and small-town plazas; it has an energetic drive that is part of both low-rider culture and *quinceñera* fiestas; in an instant it is recognized, joyous, and bilingual.

Yet until Richard Steven Valenzuela amplified it and grafted a buoyant rock-and-roll rhythm to its traditional melody line in 1958, "La Bamba" was confined mostly to Spanish-speaking America. On a Saturday afternoon in southern California, Ritchie Valens sang in a movie theater before the screening of the feature film. Lured by the promise of hearing "the Little Richard of the San Fernando Valley," music promoter Bob Keane was in the audience. Keane had a small record company, and he quickly brought the young musician into his stable.

Among the millions who cherished the song were writer and filmmaker brothers Danny and Luis Valdez, then growing up in San Joaquin Valley. Danny Valdez recalled first hearing "La Bamba" at home on a mandolin and trumpet when he was five years old. "Our Mom and Dad would come up with spontaneous verses. It would just crack them up. 'La Bamba' has the capacity to be born and reborn over and over, yet there's a resentment among first-generation mexicanos to electrifying the song. It's like playing Gregorian chants on the synthesizer, but it's proof the song has life and the ability to transcend generations. It has the power to uplift the human spirit."

Members of the band Los Lobos went to great lengths to satisfy their curiosity about the song. In the mid-1970s they paid $35 for a bus ride to Mexico City and made their way over to the eastern Mexican state of Veracruz. "We were in this open-air bar and the musicians would come over and play 'La Bamba,'" drummer Louis Perez told me. "We were listening real close and all of a sudden they'd be making up verses about how big our nose is, making fun of the tourists. We were there for a couple of weeks. It was the time of the Chicano renaissance with all this fascination with your roots. No one in the group knew how to play harp so we substituted the mandolin. We were just kids in Levis and flannel shirts."

Since the 1950s, the C-F-G chord progression has become a basic part of the repertoire for every aspiring garage band throughout the Americas. More than 40 years after the song entered mainstream American culture, "La Bamba" has become a classic the world over. Containing elements of the African slave trade of the 16th and 17th centuries, this Mexican song entered the United States in force in the middle third of the 20th century and made it to Hollywood by the last third. To trace "La Bamba" is to reveal a sweep of history and culture that began with Spanish slavers and ends with an aisle seat in a multiplex.

∾

The song "La Bamba" began its cross-cultural odyssey in Veracruz, on Mexico's Gulf Coast, where, wrote Carlos Fuentes about his ancestral home state, "the extraordinary local bands, based on the harp and the guitar, beat a lovely sensuous rhythm throughout the night." He was writing of *jarocho* music, a style that fuses European, African, and Caribbean qualities. It is characterized by the playfulness of its lyrics and its stringed instruments—guitars in various sizes, a small harp, often a stand-up bass, and sometimes a violin. Ever since Hernán Cortés landed on the Gulf Coast in 1519, Veracruz has seen the arrival of Catholic missionaries, Caribbean pirates, African slaves, foreign troops, and seafaring traders. The result was a fusion of Spanish tradition with African, Caribbean, and native life. This mixed-blood population came to be called mestizo, and its songs, coupled with unique dances and rhythms, were known in Veracruz as jarocho-style songs. Of the hundreds and hundreds of tunes that evolved from that hybrid, "La Bamba" is the most durable.

Although its popularity is assured, "La Bamba's" origins are still unknown. The Spanish brought slaves to the Gulf Coast in the early 1600s from six parts of western Africa, including a place called Mbamba. Could "La Bamba" have been a blend of Spanish and an African tongue? Probably so, says *Sones de la tierra,* a book on Veracruz music: "The name Bamba evokes the original province of the black Congolese." A number of West African tribes, rivers, and towns are named using various forms of the word "bamba." In Veracruz the song gained local notoriety not long after a pirate named Lorencillo attacked the town in 1683, an event sung about in a late 1600s version of "La Bamba."

As veracruzano minstrels and troubadours traveled out of the region and from one Mexican town to another, "La Bamba" spread, infecting the countryside with its rhythms and song. One historian places the first recorded version of "La Bamba" in 1908. In the following decades, 250,000-watt clear-channel radio station XEW broadcast the song and other standards from Mexico City to pueblos throughout the country and beyond. It became a favorite in Garibaldi Plaza, Mexico City, which has been a musicians' gathering place since the 1920s. Starting in the late 1930s, Mexico's burgeoning film industry exploited the country's regional folk styles, often with a nightclub-cum-brothel dance scene, and Mexican composers celebrating regional traditions have woven the song into symphonic scores. By World War II, "La Bamba" had reached into every home, every cabaret and concert hall, and every movie theater in the republic.

"La Bamba" gained its widest popularity when Miguel Alemán, a Veracruz native, became Mexico's president in 1946. It was during the Alemán years that northbound migrant labor carried the song into the American border states. Wherever Alemán was received in the world, welcoming bands would strike up "La Bamba." Tropical music was in its heyday, and the instantly recognizable "La Bamba" quickly became a favorite at newly opened nightclubs in Acapulco and Tijuana. The wife of the American ambassador to Mexico, said the press, had danced to "La Bamba" at a state affair, much to the chagrin of veracruzanos, who saw their rustic ditty being taken over by high society. It became Mexico's signature song.

Mexico is a country whose capital dominates the national culture, and jarocho music has found its niche there, preserved to a healthy degree by musicians from Veracruz who weave among Mexico City's pedestrians and diners. I met Raúl Rosas Santos at El Chimbombo, where he played daily, and we drove over to his house near the airport to talk. Rosas, who came to Mexico City many years back "to play the tables," had a reputation for inventing songs on the spur of the moment.

"I am a decrepit old man," said Rosas, who appeared neither worn nor aged. "It gives me great pleasure to tell you about our folklore. I'm lacking a bit in culture, but people love our music. We make up verses on the spur of the moment, depending on what's happening, and we make it rhyme. Sometimes we tell jokes with double entendre and eroticism. We speak of politics and international events. We're like local reporters, only we do it in verse form.

"The evolution of 'La Bamba' is like an invention of Thomas Edison's—first it's rudimentary, then you begin adding things. That song has been very popular wherever I've played." Without warning, Rosas pulled out his guitar and composed a jarocho song about my visit to his home. More up to date than that he could not get.

∿

My passion for "La Bamba" has also carried me to Veracruz. Although modern inconveniences have reduced the city's tranquillity that Carlos Fuentes wrote of, the appeal of its white architecture, its warm sea breezes, and its inhabitants' gentility still set it apart from Mexico's more cosmopolitan centers. I learned during my first visits there in the 1980s that mornings are best begun at Café de la Parroquia, next to the Zócalo. The café's origins date back to the early 1800s, by which time "La Bamba" had already traveled throughout Mexico.

Despite the early hour, jarocho music is never far from veracruzano ears. Two men dressed in white walked by carrying a long marimba, then plopped it down and started playing. Believing that no day in Veracruz should begin without "La Bamba," I asked them to play the song. The delicacy of its rhythm and tone startled me; they played to the tempo of a fluttering butterfly. When the marimberos had finished "La Bamba," they proffered a small note pad listing a hundred more songs in their repertoire. I declined to choose one and paid them their three dollars. They picked up their marimba and strolled over to the next café. The nighttime sensuality that Carlos Fuentes rhapsodized about enveloped the morning as well.

Xalapa, Veracruz's capital, lay inland, two hours northwest, more than 4,000 feet above sea level. It's a university town known for its orchestra and music department, and it is filled with art galleries, coffeehouses, bookstores, and nightclubs. When I stepped off the bus, the opening lyrics to "La Bamba" greeted me: *Para bailar la bamba, se necesita una poca de gracias*—To dance la bamba, you need a little bit of grace. And elegance was in fact evident in Xalapa, especially in the persons of Sara Arróñez Ramírez, a dance instructor, and Manolo, her partner. As the song played on a cassette I carried with me, the two demonstrated the dance.

With the opening notes, Manolo's sash was unwrapped from his waist and laid on the ground. In rhythm, the two moved up and back on either side of it. Then, with her left foot, Sara reshaped the sash into something resembling a backward S. Using their feet, lifting and tugging, pulling and holding, the couple maneuvered the sash into a neatly tied bow. Manolo lifted it with his foot, grabbed one loop with one hand, and placed the other loop around Sara.

"It's easy once you get the hang of it," Sara said afterward at a nearby café, "but fewer and fewer people know how to do it."

"You know," I said in passing, "there was a very popular rock-and-roll version of 'La Bamba' in the United States."

"¡No!" she cried, as she put a hand to her face. *"¡No me diga!"* Say it ain't so!

Sara would have been less horrified by the changing lyrics to the song, as new words have been a hallmark of Veracruz music since jarocho culture emerged from the African, Spanish, and native cultural ménage à trois. At the height of the Chicano movement in the 1970s, activists sang a version called "La Bamba Chicana," with the line *Para ser Chicano, se necesita un poquito de boicot*—To be Chicano requires a little bit of boycott. Another version changes "bamba" to "bomba" and becomes an anti-nuclear bomb rendition. In the 1700s, Roman Catholic priests in Veracruz frowned on songs such as "La Bamba," which encouraged suggestive body movements and double entendre, yet today the sanctity and solemnity of religious music embraces that same song. Nowhere is this more evident than in "La Bamba" sung by the Mormon Tabernacle Choir.

The song has its place in literature, too. At the end of the novel *The Milagro Beanfield War,* set in northern New Mexico, hero Joe Mondragón conks out on the floor in sottish revery: "Stars did 'La Bamba' in his brain." It also invaded McCarthyism, according to folksinger Travis Edmonson of Arizona, who, as a West Coast folkie back then, says he was subpoenaed to a congressional hearing because he performed a foreign folk tune assumed to be about the bomb.

Hoping to find a point of contention, I asked musicians in Mexico if they were annoyed that so many gringos had profited handsomely from one of their most cherished folk songs. Not one of them fell for my ploy—on the contrary, most seemed pleased that their song had shown so much elasticity. In the States, Travis Edmonson acknowledged his debt to Mexico by sending his royalties to the mariachis' union headquartered in Guadalajara. "They'd distribute the money to the musicians of Veracruz. That struck me as right."

Trips to Veracruz have always satisfied my bambaddiction, but none more thoroughly than when I go to Tlacotalpan, a river village in the south of the state and a bit inland that dates to pre-Columbian times. My goal is the Feria de la Candelaria, an annual early February celebration in many ways akin to a county fair. In Tlacotalpan, it is said, you're either a saint or a sinner, which always makes for an interesting visit. All of Tlacotalpan, observes Mexican author Elena Poniatowska, speaks in verse. Never have I seen a town with so many rocking chairs, almost always in use. Their movement, Poniatowska writes, "goes from the past to the future, back and forth, back and forth, the wood creaking in complaint, but never breaking." The town, designated a UNESCO World Heritage City in 1998, is one of the best places to hear unadulterated jarocho music.

Live performances are the high point of the Feria, whether on the official stage, impromptu on a side-street wooden platform, or spontaneous in the crowded Tlalcotalpan cantinas. On the formal stage, musicians sang the songs of Mexico and of countries to its south. Stone-faced elderly women from the countryside danced to roving jarocho musicians on the informal wooden platform; bowls of water placed beneath the wooden planks magnified the sound of the dancers' resonance. And in a dank bar that had no name, a lone campesino silenced the crowd by singing "La Bamba" a cappella. The man looked the embodiment of generations of veracruzanos, starting with the first African slaves from Mbamba. The timbre of his voice provided its own accompaniment. He stood expressionless, rocking back and forth on his bare feet, his eyes rolled into the past. He finished to a smattering of applause, drained his beer, and left as the rest of us returned to our conversations. "La Bamba" never sounded the same to me after that. If the heart of "La Bamba" still beats anywhere, it has to be in Tlacotalpan.

∾

If tracing the roots of songs reveals both history and legend, then we should listen closely to two popular Southwest tunes. One is a little-known George Jones tearjerker, "Open Pit Mine"; the other is the well-known Marty Robbins cowboy ballad, "El Paso."

Neither has the far-ranging landscape or renown of "La Bamba," yet each addresses a well-defined audience—and both embrace a universal theme. Together they cross the borders of jealousy and the frontiers of love.

"Open Pit Mine" takes place in the adjoining Arizona mining communities of Clifton and Morenci. The song tells of a Clifton miner who catches his wife with another man; he kills her and buries her at the bottom of the local copper mine, then shoots himself. "Open Pit Mine" was released in 1962; in its best week, the song rose only as high as No. 13 on the country-music charts.

In Clifton and Morenci, however, the George Jones ballad became a classic. The description of the two neighboring Arizona towns, their ambience, and the drudgery of working in the Phelps Dodge mine struck a responsive chord with the folks of Greenlee County. In the ensuing years, this chord has echoed up and down Chase Creek, along the San Francisco River, and through the canyons.

From Morenci, Arizona, where the copper mines glow,
I can see Clifton in the canyon below.
In Clifton lived Rosie, we danced and we dined,
On the money I made in the open pit mine.

The story line in "Open Pit Mine" is strong and convincing, if a bit melodramatic at the end, yet who in a mining camp has never filled the gaps between shifts with passion, jealousy, and rage? Something about the lyrics—not to mention George Jones's plaintive voice—suggests intimate knowledge of the mining towns and their temperament, their fatalism.

Clifton, in the canyon below, was settled by prospectors look-ing for gold in the 1870s and '80s; it was named for either an early prospector or the fact that it was surrounded by cliffs. Morenci, with its company store and housing up above, was named long ago by the owner of the Detroit Copper Company, one of the com-panies that through buyouts, mergers, and takeovers over the years led to ownership by Phelps Dodge. It was probably called Morenci for a like-named Michigan town. The pit, begun shortly before World War II, became so big by 1960 that workers living in Morenci were relocated so the pit could be widened even further. The company offices are up in Morenci; the union hall was down in Clifton. It is an isolated area with long memories of family feuds, union struggles, and natural disasters.

I loved my sweet Rosie, and she loved me too.
There was nothing for Rosie that I wouldn't do.
Her hugs and her kisses they were something divine.
Gave me reason for working the open pit mine.

"Open Pit Mine" was a favorite in local bars during the devas-tating strike that began in the summer of 1983. The union was so insistent and Phelps Dodge so resistant that by late August Governor Bruce Babbitt—later to become Secretary of the Interior—sent in the National Guard to pacify the workers with tear gas. To make matters far worse, the San Francisco River suffered terrible floods from that year's autumn rains. Many of Clifton's houses and busi-nesses washed away; without jobs and homes, many families left.

Strike demands, which hinged on an automatic cost-of-living adjustment, were masterfully manipulated by Phelps Dodge's historically intransigent approach to settlement. Scabs soon filled union positions, and many striking miners, their bank accounts evaporating, reluctantly refilled their old positions on company terms. Local 616 had been part of the militant Mine, Mill & Smelter Workers union of the 1940s and '50s, a proud and combative organization that worked aggressively on behalf of its members. In the early 1960s, the militant Mine-Mill local recast itself as a tamer Steel Workers local. By the time of the strike, America's labor movement had endured unwelcomed seismic shifts, changes felt in Clifton-Morenci and throughout Western mining camps. P-D machinations so debilitated Local 616 that by February 1986 the union was decertified. The entire drama became a textbook case of Reagan-era labor-management relations, in which strikers were often summarily fired and replaced on management terms. Where once ten labor unions held sway, now there were none. Throughout the whole ordeal, unemployed, laid off, and striking miners passed the time in local bars. George Jones's "Open Pit Mine" was the perfect cry-in-your-beer tune.

While I was out walking with my Rosie one day.
We passed a store window with rings on display.
I bought those she wanted, how they really did shine.
Spent the money I saved from that open pit mine.

For a few days I made it my professional duty to visit as many Clifton and Morenci bars as I could to find the story behind the music. Did anyone know the songwriter? The circumstances that brought it about? And who was Rosie?

"It was written by a guy who lives here," Zina Mitchell told me from behind the bar at the Cave in Clifton.

"A guy who came up here with his daddy from Globe wrote it," I learned from Lillian Griffin, who managed the bowling alley in Morenci. "He delivered *The Arizona Republic* years ago. We met him through CB radio."

The Open Pit, a Morenci bar whose very name hinted broadly at details, disappointed me most. The song has been off and on The Open Pit's jukebox for years, and no one knew anything about it. Most people in Clifton and Morenci embraced the song, but it had gone from topical music to uncertain legend.

The bartender at the P-D Motel on Burro Alley knew a bit. "Supposedly it was written by a fellow who worked here." He sent me to a heavy-machine operator, who swore that it was written by someone named Gentry. "I heard he sold it to George Jones for $3,000. Gentry used to work here."

Finally I dropped by El Rey on Chase Creek during happy hour, though patrons of this Clifton bar of union holdouts had little to be happy about. No George Jones on their jukebox, either. Despite the notoriety the song gave the area, the discouraging fact was that just a couple of years after the strike, you couldn't find "Open Pit Mine" at any bar in Clifton or Morenci.

Her love would bring heartbreak, that I would soon learn.
Cause she would two-time me, when my back was turned.
Rosie would go dancing and drink the red wine,
While I worked like a slave at the open pit mine.

When I mentioned "Open Pit Mine" at El Rey the fellow down the bar looked up, eyes narrowed in fearful suspicion. You'd think I had asked for a Coors (a brew then under boycott for its labor practices). "Sure, I remember that song," Pete Montoya said. "Why do you want to know?" Assured that my intentions were honorable, he took the stool next to me. "There was a girl named Rosie who lived in Clifton. The guy was a white guy who wore a black hat. He worked in Morenci. Everything in the song was the truth. It was real."

"Yeah?" I gave him a squint of skepticism.

Montoya, a 50-year-old retired diesel-locomotive repairman for P-D, nodded. He had spent virtually his entire life in the area and assured me he knew what he was talking about.

"You know that song?" he called out to Norma at the far end of the bar.

"Naaah," Norma replied. "I'm not into honky music."

Montoya turned back to me. "The people around here know who he was singing about. Rosie was a Mexican. She'd go to the Western Tavern and the Wagon Wheel. She probably came in here, too. She used to go out with Anglos. She was screwin' them. They're the ones to ask." I bought Pete a Michelob. "The guy who wrote it was from Oklahoma or someplace. He was a redneck."

Montoya left for the men's room. The visit must have sobered him up somewhat, because on his return he started to undermine his own story. "I don't know if it's folklore or what," he said when he sat back down. "I heard from people that it was the truth. It could be a bunch of b.s., but I believe it."

One night I caught Rosie on her rendezvous.
She was huggin' and kissin' with somebody new.
It was there that I shot her while their arms were entwined.
Then I buried her deep in that open pit mine.

Word spread that an out-of-towner was asking about the song, and the next day I got a call. Speak with Ray Buford, I was advised.

Ray Buford knew it all, it seemed; plus, he had the 45, which listed a D.T. Gentry as its writer. "The boy who wrote it was a visitor," Buford, a retired mechanic in the same open pit mine, said with finality. "I met him when he was out here in '55. His cousin J.T. was a brakeman. J.T. said he wrote it and gave it to his brother because he had better connections."

And Rosie?

"Well, she was married at the time. She was precocious," Ray said with a laugh. "Nobody actually got killed on account of her, but there were quite a few fights. She was an Anglo. She's a pretty nice woman, just a little rank. When her husband would go to work on the p.m., why, she'd leave the house, too." He chuckled at the memory. "By the way, I'd appreciate it if you didn't use his name. She's still married to the same fellow. He never knew."

At the overlook on U.S. 191—for most of its life called 666— D. T. Gentry could peer far into the pit, now about three miles wide and 2,000 feet deep. From the No. 10 dump, he could see Clifton below.

At sunset the mine's walls take on a rust hue. Gargantuan trucks crawl up and down the sides to dump their loads of copper-rich dirt and return for more. The pit is so deep you can barely hear their motors, much less spy the ghosts of Clifton's forlorn husband and his runaround wife.

I finally tracked down D. T. Gentry, the man whose lyrics had survived strikes and floods, rumors and myths. He lives in a small town in Indiana. In 1952, 24-year-old Delbert Gentry headed west from his native Arkansas, looking for work. "I stopped in Clifton for a few days and stayed with friends. I was so struck by the area that I applied for a job at the mine," he recounted over the phone in a rich Ozark accent. "They wouldn't take me on account of my size. I was five-three and weighed 110. I went on to California, where I picked cotton and worked in the potato patches. I made enough to get back home to Arkansas."

Yet something about Clifton stayed with him. Gentry moved north a few years later and found work at the Fisher Body Plant making car frames for General Motors, where he worked until his retirement. During convalescence from minor surgery, he wrote out his copper-miner's Romeo and Juliet. It had been taking shape in his mind ever since that brief stop in Clifton nine years earlier.

In the summer of 1961, Delbert Gentry went to a George Jones concert and stood in the autograph line afterward. "Would you listen to a song if I sent it to you?" he asked the star. Jones gave him his address and a friend of Gentry's made a reel-to-reel demo tape of "Open Pit Mine."

"I sent it off and got a contract by return mail September 1, 1961. It was a dream come true. Every six months or so I get a small check. Sometimes it'll be shut off for a couple of years, then I'll get another one."

What about his cousin J.T., the brakeman in Clifton? And the white guy in the black hat? And the job delivering newspapers? And meeting the bowling-alley manager through CB? And Rosie the wench—Anglo or Mexican, take your pick—at the Western Tavern and the Wagon Wheel? And her cuckolded husband who never knew? And and and...?

"I was only in Clifton for a few days. I never met anyone there named Rosie; the name just fit the song. I never had any relatives there, either."

I took a look at my future and what did I see.
There was nothing but trouble a-waiting for me.
But on the sun's next risin' I'll be satisfied.
'Cause they'll find me there sleeping by my sweet Rosie's side.

～

The enormous pit at Morenci declares that mining dominates the area. El Paso, a five-hour drive away, proclaims its mining history with two enormous smelter stacks at the city's west end. The longest stretch of that drive takes you through New Mexico on an interstate once named The Border Friendship Route, now called The Pearl Harbor Memorial Highway. Signs for El Paso, the most populated American city on the border, with well over 600,000 residents, start hundreds of miles away. Every time a mileage sign comes into view, I unconsciously hum the tune to the 1959 Marty Robbins hit, "El Paso." As I get closer I start singing the words, and by the time I see EL PASO 20 I am literally shouting the lyrics.

"El Paso" tells the tale of a cowboy who falls madly in love with Felina, a flirtatious dancer at Rosa's Cantina.

One night a wild young cowboy came in,
Wild as the West Texas wind.
Dashing and daring a drink he was sharing
With wicked Felina, the girl that I loved.
So in anger I challenged his right for the love of this maiden.
Down went his hand for the gun that he wore.
My challenge was answered. In less than a heartbeat
The handsome young stranger lay dead on the floor.

Only two verses into the song and already we have insane jealousy, interracial love, a barroom shoot-out, and a dead body. The cowboy— *"shocked by the foul evil deed I had done"*—runs out the back door, steals the fastest-looking horse, and rides *"just as fast as I could from the West Texas town of El Paso / Out to the badlands of Old Mexico."*

Now we have a murderer and a horse thief on our hands, who, in the best tradition of borderland outlaws, crosses the frontier to escape punishment. (The song's original lyric has him ride off to Old Mexico; this was revised to New Mexico on the record. We'll stay with the original.)

Despite the considerable obstacles preventing their reunion, the cowboy longs to see Felina. *"My love is stronger than my fear of death.... Maybe tomorrow a bullet will find me. Tonight nothing's worse than this pain in my heart"* and he saddles up for his fateful return to El Paso. As he begins his final approach, a posse surrounds him. His only choice is a suicidal dash for his loved one: *"Shouting and shooting I can't let them catch me. I have to make it to Rosa's back door."*

Finally:

I see a white puff of smoke from the rifle,
I feel the bullet go deep in my chest.
From out of nowhere Felina has found me,
Kissing my cheek as she kneels by my side.
Cradled by two loving arms that I'll die for,
One little kiss and Felina goodbye.

"El Paso" is an oater of Shakespearean dimension, but to true aficionados of borderland mythology, many gaps remained in its story. Where did Felina come from? What drew her to Rosa's? Marty Robbins obliged these devotees in 1966 with "Felina from El Paso," a sequel that gained little popularity. (Felina's story: At 17 she runs away to Santa Fe from the shack where she was raised, and learns that her good looks can get her anything she desires. A year later she takes the stage to El Paso, where she puts on a form-fitting black satin dress and finds work as a dancer at Rosa's. After a year, during which men continue to slobber over her, the young cowboy comes in and for six weeks they become a couple.)

"El Paso" ends with her lover's death. "Felina from El Paso" completes the tragedy:

Quickly she grabbed the six-gun that he wore.
And screaming in anger and placing the gun to her breast,
"Bury us deep and maybe we'll find peace!"
Pulling the trigger she fell 'cross the dead cowboy's chest.

If the songs had historical validity, then the drama would have unfolded on the west side of town, most likely on the edge of a barrio where both Mexicans and Anglos could frequent the cantina. The

Rio Grande must be nearby so the cowboy can quickly ride back and forth. And Rosa's must be near the bottom of a hill *("...here I am on the hill overlooking El Paso, I can see Rosa's Cantina below.")*.

I spent hours driving the streets of El Paso until I found the truth: Rosa's Cantina lives.

It sits on Doniphan Road near Sunland Park Race Track in a curious stretch of land where the states of Texas, New Mexico, and Chihuahua all bump into each other. Any one of the three states is only steps away from the other two. A cowboy could gallop from Rosa's across the Rio Grande into Old—or New—Mexico in less than a minute.

At a distance, Rosa's appears a forgotten building from another era. White paint covers its adobe walls. Unpaved parking spaces adjoin the building. The bar's name, spelled out in large red plastic letters in front and again in wrought iron on the front door, is all that indicates life within.

Rosa's Cantina, El Paso

Inside, Rosa's Cantina is magnificent. The spacious, dimly lit barroom has enough room for Felina and a hundred others to dance deep into the night. Paintings tracing El Paso's history cover part of the west wall. The opposite wall sports a string of chili peppers and a Bud Lite football poster shadowed by a ten-point buck. Trophies won by Rosa's entry in the Upper Valley Little League line another. Below an American flag, a cowboy hat, and a poster of a young Lucha Villa, a singer from Guadalajara, sits the jukebox. Yes, "El Paso" is there: punch 60-11.

Roberto Zubia, an industrious and friendly man born in 1923, four years after the building itself came into being, bought the bar in the mid-1950s. A few weeks later he sat down with some friends and Trini and Rosa, two sisters who worked there, to come up with a new name to go with the new ownership. A friend suggested naming it for one of the sisters, and someone else thought "Rosa" went well with "cantina." The story turns to conjecture at this point: They—the ubiquitous "they"—say that Marty Robbins was passing through town not long after, drove by the bar, and kept the name in mind. C&W celebrity has sanctified the bar ever since.

At the time, Roberto worked two jobs to support his family: in maintenance at a downtown hotel and at the cantina until the bar started to break even. When someone pointed him out to me on my first visit in the late 1970s, I asked him if he was, in fact, the owner. "Rosa, hah!" came the reply. "She owns me!"

Rosa's opens for lunch daily with meals prepared by Roberto's wife, Anita, and two younger generations of the family. Each table has a handwritten menu listing specials of the day such as Chili Con Queso, Short Ribs Soaked in Red Chile, Brisket Tostadas, or Hamburger Steak. The meals come with rice, refried beans, soup, white corn tortillas, and iced tea—and each costs $3.50 complete. The price has doubled since I first ate there.

Regular customers include mailmen from a post office not far from the bar, workers from the power plant down the street, and family friends. Even with the nearby ASARCO (American Smelting and Refining Company) plant shut down, some of its former workers still come around. In the old days, workers from ASARCO, which processed zinc, lead, copper, and antimony, kept the place lively. "It's a good bar, Rosa's," maintenance foreman Jesús Martínez told me back then. "We always come here. After a day at ASARCO we need to." And owner Roberto spoke of the rich history he had seen unfold in the area.

"You're going all the way to Tijuana?" he asked. "Tell me, does Tijuana have a history? I don't think so. Not like here. That's why they call it El Paso. Let me show you something."

We hopped in my car and drove a mile to a flat stretch of barren land directly beneath the ASARCO stacks. The Rio Grande was at our feet, no more than 50 feet wide and only a few feet deep. "This is where I grew up," Roberto explained with affection. "About 900 people used to live here. In the early 1970s, the last of the houses was torn down. Everyone called the community Smeltertown.

"There was only one industry in Smelter in the old days: smuggling. My daddy was involved in it, and so was everyone else. The Mexicans used to bring whiskey and tequila across by the sackful in *latas,* the kind of cans you store lard in. Smelter families would hide the booze in their homes waiting for it to be picked up.

"The Mexican smugglers had to contend with the *fiscales* (law enforcement officers) to get the contraband across. Sometimes there were three-day fights between the smugglers and the fiscales. People would die, but the contraband usually got through. Night-time was best for moving the goods.

"The whole scene was crazy. U.S. customs agents would try to catch smugglers who got by the Mexican authorities. If the smug-glers killed an American customs man, they'd drag his body back to the Mexican side and leave it there. If the contrabandistas killed one of the fiscales, his body would be brought over to the U.S. side. In the mornings we'd all go down to the riverside and see who was killed and who survived. I was only nine when Prohi-bition ended, but I remember these things. Many corridos were written about the smugglers and how brave they were. I have one on the jukebox, it's called 'El Contrabando de El Paso.' Today the smugglers bring drugs across. I don't like that."

Back at the bar, Roberto played "El Contrabando de El Paso." Anita, busy arranging tables for a private wedding party that night, came over to show me a souvenir: a day-sheet from *When You Comin' Back Red Ryder?* The interior of Rosa's had been used for some scenes in the movie. Another film—*El Paso, City by the Rio Grande*—was shot in El Paso a few years later at the behest of the city's Visitors and Convention Bureau. An advertising agency hired Marty Robbins to write the title song and narrate the script. The movie opens with Robbins in front of an old, abandoned adobe building with a crooked sign that says "Rosa's Cantina." The film boasts El Paso's history of bandits and barroom shootouts, balancing them with modern tourist attractions to draw future business. The title song, the last in Marty Robbins's Felina Trilogy, was a syrupy rehash of the original "El Paso" story—this time from the perspective of a man flying over the city, imagining that in his former life he was Felina's cowboy paramour.

Roberto had heard about the tourist film when it was under production: "They went to the racetrack; they went to Ranger Peak; and they went to the bullring in Juárez. But they didn't come here." Roberto looked around his cantina and shrugged. "I guess this isn't the image they wanted."

Both Roberto and Anita play along with the guessing game—which came first, the bar or the song?—but usually they leave that to their customers, who play "El Paso" some 25 times a week. These days when tourists come in, Mario Gallegos or one of the other regulars will take them on a tour of the place. Gallegos, a mail carrier in his early 50s who played on a Rosa's Little League team as a youth, shows them the back door through which the cowboy ran, Mt. Cristo Rey (*"the hill overlooking El Paso"*) just south of Rosa's on the fringe of Cormac MacCarthy country, part in New Mexico, part in Old Mexico, the Rio Grande itself—and, on the wall, a full-size framed portrait of Felina that someone sent Roberto from New York. It's a convincing painting of a demure Spanish señorita wearing a mantilla and clasping a fan. Until someone stole it, the frame had a metal plaque attached to it that simply said "Felina."

Both "Rosa's Cantina" and "Open Pit Mine" end with their lovers dead. The emotional turmoil mixed with the mythic notoriety give extra energy to the songs' Southwestern personalities. Even Roberto Zubia is not immune. Despite all the good-natured folderol about the Felina trilogy, Roberto confesses to some of the same nostalgia his visitors proclaim: "Sometimes when I'm sitting in here at the bar, alone, and one of those songs comes on, I cry."

HOLLYWOOD GOES SOUTHWEST

A
rt dispels the romance of the Southwest while heralding its strengths and unveiling its sins. The late Santa Fe author Stan Steiner, who wrote numerous books on the American West, told of the Hispanic family in northern New Mexico who, one lovely Saturday morning, headed to town for the weekly shopping. Their pickup got stuck in an arroyo, and try as they might, the family couldn't get the truck to budge. A few minutes later some friends heading in the opposite direction likewise found themselves immobile in the same wash. Everyone pushed and pulled, shoveled dirt and moved rocks, but to no avail. A few more pickups pulled up behind the ones lodged in the dry riverbed, and soon a line of a half-dozen trucks had formed in both directions behind the first two. The men spent the day sipping beer and swapping stories under some cottonwood trees up the hill. Their wives did the same down in the arroyo. The kids played on the trucks, jumping on the hoods and hiding in the beds. Their dogs lay on the road in the high mountain sun.

Later that afternoon an Anglo drove up in his Buick sedan, walked down to the lead trucks, and within five minutes figured out how to get them rolling again. "I can get your pickups out," the white man announced triumphantly as he walked up the hill, interrupting the men lounging under the cottonwood trees. Whereupon they beat the crap out of him.

"Whenever I tell that story to an all-Anglo audience," Steiner recounted, "it's met by stone silence. When the audience is half-and-half, there are titters. But when I'm talking to an all-Hispanic group, they just crack up."

It's rare to find such honest and impolite humor about race and class in the public domain. The troublesome and eternal theme of discrimination seldom surfaces in mainstream art—all the more reason, then, to accent the importance of two movies, both filmed in New Mexico, that deal candidly with both.

This is the state that license plates justifiably laud as the "Land of Enchantment," where unemployment and poverty soar as high as the Sangre de Cristo range and public education funding dips as low as the Rio Grande Gorge. In the small towns north of Santa Fe, where some residents can boast of ancestors dating back more than 300 years, the intrusion of outsiders has always meant trouble. Tradition and suspicion go hand in hand. It was here in this magical land with its homemade problems that author John Nichols set his terrific 1974 comedic fiction, *The Milagro Beanfield War,* and here, in the fictional village of Milagro, that Robert Redford directed a movie 12 years later based upon Nichols's classic novel.

Virtually from the day *The Milagro Beanfield War* was published, filmmakers sought to convert its diverse and quirky characters and subplots from the printed page to the silver screen. The story line, which works well in type, seemed too unwieldy for film. It wove too many elements at once: In addition to race it had greed, water rights, weapons, class consciousness, sexuality, land development, cultural clumsiness, government, and tradition. Only after repeated attempts by screenwriters did a script adaptation emerge that could fulfill requirements for a full-blown Hollywood production and still hint at the essential power and zaniness of the original book.

John Nichols

Milagro was Hollywood's first big-budget film focusing on Chicano culture to compete for 120 minutes of middle America's attention. Other films involving Latino culture have either been negative stereotypes—bikers, gangs, drug traffickers—or have been suppressed, such as *Salt of the Earth,* or are slightly outside the mainstream, such as *Zoot Suit* and *The Ballad of Gregorio Cortez.* The *Milagro* cast, reflecting the book, was primarily Latino and included extras from the region where the story took place. To call it a "Chicano movie" could be misleading, for the story line dealt with humanity more than race. Further, many in northern New Mexico see themselves as descended from Spaniards (hence Hispanos) rather than Mexicans (hence Chicano). Mixed into the movie's plot are Latino *vendidos*—sellouts—and virtuous Anglos. The Southwest's powerful racial mix makes a strong argument for ignoring heritage entirely and focusing on righteousness and honor. To the extent that *Milagro* took an "us versus them" attitude, it's an old and honorable one: have-nots versus haves, the powerless against the elite.

~

The lungs and skin notice you're there first, even before the eyes and ears. A sunrise snap in the crystalline air, the invigorating nip of a twilight breeze, a bracing chill 'neath high mountain shadows. Ed Abbey was right when he said that nature in northern New Mexico can be religion itself. And like all religions, sanctimony and squabbles are never far.

As squabbles go, this one was entirely appropriate. In the location of choice—the 250-year-old village of Chimayo—not everybody was thrilled with the idea of having a movie shot through their midsection. Redford Schmedford, some people simply didn't want the movie personality and his multimillion-dollar budget in their town. In all, 17 landowners had to give permission for the movie to invade their preserve, but only 14 relented; three others—including a Santa Fe school principal who lived in Chimayo—asked for more money than the production company was paying their neighbors, and *Milagro* pulled out of Chimayo before it moved in.

This upset David Ortega, the town's *patrón,* whose ancestors had settled there in 1696. Ortega ran the family gift shop, which features locally produced weavings and pottery. What happened? I asked. "Ah, some creeps stopped them from coming in. Most of the people wanted them. They would have cleaned up the area and fixed the ditch, something it sorely needed. It would have been very good for business."

Next door another merchant spoke of the troubles that characterize Chimayo. "We've had purse snatchings and such. Tourists aren't exactly welcome in parts of the village. It's practically lawless here. The sheriff's department has almost given up on it."

Chimayo's plaza can deceive at first. In fact, a visitor can drive down the dirt road bisecting it without knowing he or she is in the plaza at all. Unlike plazas traditionally associated with Mexican villages, the Plaza de Cerro is more like a presidio, first established under Spanish rule to encircle the village and protect it from Indians. Houses, many in splendid decay on the outside, line the perimeter of the plaza in this sparsely populated rural town. When I visited, local youths lounged in front yards downing beer, fixing engines, listening to the radio. The heart of the plaza resembled Armante Córdova, the *Milagro* character whose continued breathing defied logic and medicine. Weeds sprang from every crack in the ground. An overgrown and underused ditch sliced through one part of the plaza. The Placita Game Room had long since been boarded up. Crumbling adobe cubicles took up one of the plaza's sides. An old chapel, still in occasional use, anchored another.

On a windy, autumn weekday I could find only one person in the plaza, a man in his 70s sawing firewood for the coming winter. He piled his wood near some tall windbreaks. A dog rested alongside him. Only chirping birds and my impolite questions broke the silence of his quiet afternoon. His wife, walking with the aid of a cane, emerged from their long yellow house.

"The majority of the people here really didn't want it," the old man said of using Chimayo as the film's location. He acknowledged that he was part of that majority. "But I was just one person. They said they would take that wall down over there"— he gestured with his handsaw—"and later rebuild it, but how would the town benefit from that? Old people live here. It would bring turmoil to our lives. Could we sell food to the movie people? No, they have that catered. Could we be extras? They said we'd have to travel all the way to Santa Fe (35 miles south) and join the Screen Actors Guild. I really didn't want to meet Robert Redford." He smiled faintly, nodded slightly, and resumed sawing.

Chimayo's loss was Ruben Tafoya's gain, and Truchas, where land and cinema were more compatible, got Redford's brass ring. On the four-mile drive east from one Rio Arriba County village to the other, "butterflies smashed against the windshield in lovely patterns," as John Nichols described it in his book. As the patrón of Truchas, Tafoya stood to profit most. The land on which the actual bean field was filmed?—Tafoya's acreage, leased to the filmmakers; the wood to build the set from scratch?—from Tafoya's lumberyard. Much of the one million dollars to be spent in Truchas passed through Tafoya's cash register. He bragged that his son earned $20 an hour as set carpenter, about four times the 1986 norm in this town of 1,000.

A set used in the filming of Milagro Beanfield War *in Truchas, New Mexico*

Ruben Tafoya wore a grease-stained Exxon shirt in his general store. "See this?" He pointed to the inside cover of his personal copy of *The Milagro Beanfield War.* There were two signatures, one from the Santa Fe high school principal who effectively blocked the filming in Chimayo, and below that, "Thanks for all your help, Ruben. *Robert Redford.*"

Tafoya sold 200 copies of the paperback in the first few weeks of filming. He put a Truchas, N. Mex. stamp in each one. "You can buy the book here or bring in your own copy and I'll stamp it. Free of charge. I've also got *Milagro* T-shirts." The shirts, silk-screened locally and available exclusively through Tafoya's shop, sold well until a cease-and-desist letter from the movie's lawyer halted his freelance production.

The conflict in *Milagro* came about when Joe Mondragón, a local jackass-of-all trades, impulsively irrigated his fallow .7-acre bean field with water from an irrigation channel, water that would have benefited a polyester developer—water that, under an old pact, had been denied to salt-of-the-earth farmers. Joe's petty act of ornery disobedience sent a medicine ball of fear into the gut of bola-tied business and political muckety-mucks, and very quickly state undercover cops and their hired goons tried to intimidate and sabotage what they perceived as a nascent rebellion.

The good people of Milagro—and some of the bad—overreacted, which of course encouraged the developer and law enforcers to do likewise until the inevitable clash. Mixed into the fray was VISTA volunteer Herbie Goldfarb, whose pitiful helplessness provided comic relief; Kyril Montana, the cool and collected state undercover cop whose methodical game plan for ending the rebellion met failure; Nancy Mondragón, Joe's strong wife, who pushed him when he needed prodding and pulled him when he went too far; and of course Joe. Other roles included Armante Córdova, the wise old fool who outlived three generations of his own family; the state governor; and Charlie Bloom, the rural lawyer whose cowardice was never sufficient to run away from a conflict but whose convictions were too weak to seize upon one. Nichols has always had a good ear, and in *Milagro* he handed Redford a wide range of characters whose names themselves roll around the tongue: Gomersindo Leyba, Tranquilino Jeantette, and the hero of a bygone fight with the feds, Snuffy Ledoux, whose name Nichols made into one of the most wonderfully sounding battle cries in American literature; "¡Que viva Snuffy!"

These characters and others run amok through *Milagro,* supported by a cast of lesser folk. Mangy and stubborn farm animals wander through the story, often metaphors for nothing more than mangy and stubborn farm animals. Rights to irrigate small fields from Rio Grande water have been disputed practically since the hoe was invented, and *Milagro* simply takes the political issue and gives it a human face. *Cara de tú, cuerpo de usted* (sweet face, hard body). What distinguishes *Milagro,* however, is how the characters complement the sly interplay of petty miracles and mischievous angels, cockeyed legends and half-baked visions. Race plays a role, sometimes muted, often implied, but never too far from the action. Class, on the other hand, is sometimes out loud, often explicit, and like the American kestrel, always hovering just above the center.

Attracting the most attention on and off the movie set was mechanic and plumber Ruby Archuleta, the operator of Ruby's Body Shop and Pipe Queen, who circulated a petition supporting Joe's bean field and led a small guerrilla band. Ruby was played by Sonia Braga, the Brazilian actress best known for her role in

Dona Flor and Her Two Husbands; her forays into downtown Santa Fe, where she maintained a two-bedroom townhouse, drew considerable notice.

Curiously, Santa Fe—the longest continually occupied capital in the Americas—has in almost 400 years developed only one style of architecture: clunky, brown, flat-roofed, thick-walled, presidio-style adobe buildings with deep wall niches, honeycomb fireplaces, and exposed ceiling beams. Although this design has its undeniable appeal, street after street and hill after hill of repetitive Santa Fe style—what one historian calls an "illusion of authenticity"—does tend to get tedious. Originally this was the design of simple mud houses for very poor folks, but recent generations of monied arrivistes have adapted the traditional heritage of those they've displaced. Braga's leased townhouse was in a condo development of those long-ago mud-house motifs gone chic.

Not far away at an exclusive hat shop near the Plaza, Braga tried on model after model, intently studying herself in the mirror. Finally she decided on a black Borsalino. With her black wraparound sunglasses, sequined black satin shirt, black leather pants, and lush black hair, the elegant Italian fedora looked stunning on her. She returned a few days later to pick up her newly blocked hat, and the hatter asked if she'd like her name embossed in gold lettering on the inside band. "Yes," she replied. "And make it *Mister* Sonia Braga."

"*Mister* Sonia Braga? Is that right?"

"Yes," she answered. "I'm not getting enough respect around here."

If Braga wasn't getting enough respect, certainly her character Ruby was. At her townhouse Braga told me about Ruby, whose role in the book had been expanded for her in the movie. "She's tough. She's very strong. She protects the land like a mother. But she's not a feminist. Ruby is not independent, not at all. She survives, but she depends on everybody. When she tries to collect petitions in the streets, she doesn't treat the old men any different from the others. In the back of my mind, I'm the same as Ruby."

Sonia Braga got up to stir some vegetable soup she was cooking. She wore white tights and a white knee-length T-shirt with rolled-up three-quarter sleeves. Her matching necklace and earrings were both very Santa Fe blue turquoise. Her braided hair reached her waist. She returned with a Diet Coke and a Winston for herself and some red wine for me.

"In Bahia it's traditional to wear white on Fridays. Everybody does it. Bahia is such a wonderful place. Europe is nice, but Bahia is better. In Bahia the people are slower paced than they are here. They have time to listen to you. They tell you stories. That's where Jorge Amado is from. He's our national hero and one of my best friends. I love him and his wife. All his roles for women are wonderful. Although I've acted in many of his works, I haven't read any of them. I trust him to tell me about each role. Here, let me pour you some more wine." I think Sonia Braga was trying to get me drunk.

"In Brazil they will love *Milagro*. In the States the story is a fantasy. For us it's our day-by-day. It's the way things happen in Brazil. There they dance, sing, and guard the spirits. The spirits come to earth to talk to us. Miracles and miracles. I think people in a lot of countries will recognize themselves in the characters. It is universal."

The receding sunlight on the hills radiated a lovely red, and Braga remarked upon the natural beauty of New Mexico, the light, the mountains, and the comfortable chill in the air. "You know," she said softly, "today was lovely. It was so beautiful I went out for a walk by myself. It was a wonderful day to shoot pool."

Robert Redford, Stan Steiner observed, walked around Santa Fe disguised as Robert Redford. Barflies bragged about spotting his silver Porsche. He's seen jogging at dawn near St. John's College. No, he's secreted in an old adobe north of town. Wait, didn't we see him take a room at La Fonda? Redford and his producer Moctezuma Esparza chose the best time of the year to film in northern New Mexico, after the final summer tourists had gone and before the first ski bums arrived. These were, as John Nichols titled one of his books, the last beautiful days of autumn.

When *Milagro*'s dénouement was filmed at Ruben Tafoya's Hollywood bean field east of Truchas, the movie's entire cast gathered for the film's final confrontation and victory celebration. To kill time, the New Mexican *Milagro* extras started strumming their guitars, improvising lyrics and tunes. The Hollywood actors joined in and, with neither script nor direction, the entire cast spontaneously danced to their miraculous bean-field triumph. Redford alerted the camera to start rolling. When he was satisfied with the footage, he yelled, "Cut!" The filming stopped, but the actors and musicians in the field ignored him and danced on.

∾

Another New Mexico movie tells the world about gritty strengths and corporate sins in the Southwest. This one starred an improbably cohesive mix of underground miners and Hollywood lefties. The movie would not have taken place without a militant labor union, and once the early 1950s film had come and gone, its romance lingered on. I inhaled a trace of it when I traveled to the flatland of the old Roos spread in southwest New Mexico. From where I stood I could see clusters of piñon and encina trees, and the shells of half a dozen cars lying about. The Grant County spread hadn't been mined in years. The fellow with me absentmindedly tossed rocks down one of the abandoned shafts that pockmarked the land. An autumn chill blew through his silvery-gray hair. "The bosses don't care if you're white, black, or Chicano. They're interested in cutting down on the jobs. We need a good strong union to fight the bosses. Otherwise you're a goner." Juan Chacón jammed his hands into the pockets of his heavy jacket.

That mining has dominated life in southwestern New Mexico for generations should come as no surprise; Spaniards started digging out hidden minerals two centuries ago. But that Silver City, the county seat, would become the confluence of Hollywood, Congress, militant unionists, and sniveling Red-baiters—that's a bit more unlikely. Yet between the fall of 1950 and the spring of 1954, a remarkable drama played out here in the mines, on the picket line, in front of the cameras, and behind the scenes. Generations of workers here had been tethered to the land, to extract its underground metals and take what pleasures they could from it above ground. It all converged in a strike that, thanks to some righteous filmmakers who got in over their heads, gained international notoriety. "There are a lot of people who don't believe in the union," Chacón mused. Juan Chacón, combative elder statesman of the rank-and-file labor movement, was reflecting on the verities of life in New Mexico mining camps. Chacón was slim and walked with a barely perceptible shoulder hunch. His facial lines uncrinkled when he grinned, which was often, and his eyes carried a flashbulb spark. He rocked back and forth to keep warm. "They don't know what union means."

Chacón's recollections of events decades past were as polished as fine turquoise. Back then he had played an increasingly important role in a contentious strike against a stubborn mining company and in a celebrated movie about that strike made by blacklisted Hollywood personae non gratae. The film was *Salt of the Earth,* also blacklisted, and union activist Chacón played the male lead, a union leader much like himself. He and the others walked the picket line miles away where Highway 90 and State Route 356 meet. The filming, however, took place on the Roos spread. A cult favorite for years among students of labor, feminism, cinema, and Mexican-American history, *Salt of the Earth* has since enjoyed national broadcast and video distribution.

"Young people now, they're hard to organize." Chacón chuckled dryly. "They start with good wages, sick leave, insurance, pension. I don't know why, but it's hard to get them to join the union and participate. They don't have much appreciation for the union's history." Militancy and disappointment can lead to melancholy and despondency. Chacón hadn't arrived there yet, not in the opening years of the Reagan era.

∽

June 1951. International Union of Mine, Mill and Smelter Workers Local 890 holds an emergency meeting at El Sarape, a bar they all know well. One-hundred-fifty miners had been striking against Empire Zinc in nearby Hanover since the previous October. The basic demands were simple: collar-to-collar pay—that is, pay for all time spent on the job including travel to and from the mine itself—and certain paid holidays. During the eight-month strike, Empire Zinc, a subsidiary of New Jersey Zinc and the smallest of the local mining companies, had proven intransigent. It alone among area employers refused collar-to-collar pay, countering with a nominal raise in the hourly wage. Mine-Mill wouldn't budge, and Empire, counting on the union's resources to dry up, held firm.

A proud and radical union, Mine-Mill had been expelled from the Congress of Industrial Organizations (CIO) the previous year because its officers refused to disavow Communist Party ideology. Workers from other mines, including Chacón, took part in the meeting.

Empire was tough and Local 890 was growing weaker. Some miners debated how best to settle the strike and save face, a position to which union officials in Denver were themselves slowly reconciling themselves. Yet even before that could happen, Empire devised a way to resume work: It convinced a local judge to bar unionists from picketing, as the Taft-Hartley Act permitted. With the lonely intersection of 90 and 356 clear, Mine-Mill would be helpless to prevent scabs from hiring on with impunity. Local 890 members could return, of course, but only on company terms. Otherwise they might as well belong to the Grant County chess club for all the good their strike had brought them. And so the mining community had gathered at El Sarape to plan its response.

Damn the injunction, said some, this is our strike. We've been out eight months; let's fight to the bitter end. No, said others, let's give up; if we picket tomorrow, surely we'll be arrested and the situation will be that much worse. Finally the Ladies' Auxiliary took its turn: The injunction bars only striking miners from picketing; it says nothing about their wives. We'll walk the line for you, keep the mine closed and the scabs out, and no one will be breaking the law.

The notion had been floated informally, but now out in the open it had the power of a single bolt of lightning crackling through the window. Everything before it led up to it; everything afterward led away from it. Ladies on a picket line? The more skeptical of the laborers, 30-year-old Juan Chacón among them, resisted the idea. What of possible violence? Sheriff's deputies? Company goons? Scabs? Who'll take care of the kids? Clean the house? You're not experienced strikers, you're ladies. You'll quit after a day or two. Better for us to go down fighting than have ladies do it for us.

Others were not so quick to condemn. True, women walking the line may prove disastrous, but what alternative do we have? We'll know only if we try. The women have supported us; let's let them become a fuller part of the community. Clint Jencks, Mine-Mill's full-time organizer in the area, spoke for the idea in measured tones. Juan Chacón opposed it in no uncertain terms. Local 890 President Cipriano Montoya called for a vote. The women would begin picketing the next morning. A wave of euphoria swept over the new front line, Virginia Chacón, Juan's wife of four years, included.

We had driven back to Chacón's 40-acre spread, an apple orchard near Mimbres, New Mexico, that his parents bought for $700 during the Depression. His blue-eyed father and his Tarahumara Indian mother had moved north from Chihuahua at the end of the 19th century, part of a regional mass migration impelled by economics and banditry under gathering clouds of rev- olution. By this time, Juan—Johnny to his old union buddies—was narrating history as if it were three weeks previous, not many decades. Most of the winesap, golden, and red delicious apples had been harvested the previous month, and Juan was already plotting the next year's pruning and irrigation. It was easy to see why he often came to the orchard behind his 1960s cinder-block house. Although the home had no phone, the orchard brooked no bother. Here he stripped away his daily excess and could think. Ponder. Contemplate and meditate. Guests who visited over the years knew that if Juan invited you to the orchard, you were his friend. Punto. The kid in him emerged.

As a young child, Chacón had traveled by wagon across the windswept mesas of western New Mexico with his Dad to sell the family's apple harvest at market in Arizona. When he came of age, he did what every able-bodied Grant County Mexican-American lad did: He went to work in the mines. Then came a series of jobs in war industries around the West, after which he returned home to look for work again in the mines.

"What can you do?" the personnel man at Kennecott Copper asked.

"I can weld."

"I'm sorry, but all we have for Mexicans is labor."

Chacón hired on. By the time the Ladies' Auxiliary took over the strike against Empire Zinc, Chacón was a union shop steward at Kennecott. When his wife and the other women took picket duty that next morning at Highway 90 and State Route 356, carloads of "replacement workers," as strikebreakers were politely called, were ready to drive in. Men who had picketed the previous eight months stood to the side. The women ignored paternalistic orders to leave from company officials and from a county sheriff with the lovely name of Leslie Goforth. The authorities grew more perplexed that afternoon when children from the Hanover and Santa Rita schools joined their mothers on the picket line. Empire remained shut down.

The women had goals in mind beyond pay and benefits. They insisted on hot running water, toilets, and other sanitary facilities like the Anglo miners had in their company housing. "WE WANT EQUALITY WITH OTHER WORKERS—NO MORE, NO LESS" read their signs.

"The company very quickly sensed that something new was going on," Mine-Mill organizer Clint Jencks later recalled, "that we weren't just after vacations or two bits an hour; that we were trying to reclaim a whole heritage and our whole right to human dignity. And when they became aware of that, they decided they had to stop us." Jencks, who had been sent to help the local in southwestern New Mexico by the International, stood out not just because he was blond in an unblond community, but for his ability to articulate and find consensus, to see beyond the day's agenda to the larger picture. For him, like the others involved, the strike was a defining event in his life, an adrenaline rush far greater than running rapids or scaling peaks.

Confrontations started soon. Sheriff Goforth and his deputies, paid in part by Empire Zinc, shot canisters of tear gas into the women's line to clear the way for strikebreakers. The cry *"¡No les dejan pasar!"*—Don't let them through!—went up, and when the wind finally blew the fumes away, the wives had held their line. Some *esquiroles*—scabs—simply drove in, barreling over anyone in their way; a few women were seriously injured as a result. Whenever possible, women clustered around strikebreakers' cars inching toward the mine, lifted the hoods, and ripped out the wiring. Or they'd rock the cars until they turned over. Or they'd pummel the driver, tear the hair from the passenger's head, throw rocks through the windshield, puncture tires, or toss Mexican mace—ground chili peppers—in their enemies' eyes. Women who'd never worn pants outside the home came dressed for action.

They formed car pools through the mining camps and demonstrated against the *Silver City Press* for its severely slanted coverage. Between turns on the picket line, the women napped on cots inside the strike tent. Days at a time went by with no threatening action from Empire or the ever-present sheriff's deputies, then a carload of esquiroles would approach and the women would stop it. Arrests for disorderly conduct or resisting a peace officer were common, as deputies would pluck women out of the line and haul them off to jail. For each one arrested, however, another stepped forward to take her place.

One day when more than 60 chanting picketers overflowed the Grant County jail, Sheriff Goforth offered freedom to those who agreed never to return to the strike. Everyone held fast; they were all released at nightfall. Other unions around the country sent support money and food for the New Mexico strikers' families and the women's efforts. The Ladies' Auxiliary, fueled by a sense of righteousness and momentum, assumed the vanguard in the struggle. The men, emasculated by their wives, clumsily took to home chores while keeping an ear cocked to the intersection of 90 and 356. They couldn't hear the women crochet, but the picketers' singing echoed through the mining camps. One song, "El Corrido de Empire Zinc," explained their imprisonment:

En la cárcel yo me encuentro porque sólo en huelga entré.

I'm in jail only because I joined a strike.

Los amigos que yo traigo yo se los voy a nombrar,

I'll name the friends I've brought with me,

comenzando con el Joe Hill y los héroes del movimiento.

beginning with Joe Hill and the heroes of the movement.

The Empire Zinc strikers felt they had history with them. Empire Zinc retaliated by advertising for strikebreakers in out-of-state newspapers and paying them for simply trying to crack the women's line. Though the company's reputation for inflexibility was cemented by its attitude toward the women picketing, Local 890 saw no way out of the standstill and started considering Empire's proposed settlement more seriously.

The mining community was committed to la causa because it symbolized their struggle. Some saw the dynamics of larger forces at work. The Communist Party, whose influence in Mine-Mill was significant but not dominant, helped shape Local 890's decision-making, according to one party member active in the strike. "The party was on top of every move that was made," insisted Lorenzo Torrez, now a Communist Party organizer, when I spoke with him at his Arizona home. "And it played the unifying role of explaining and clarifying events for the workers." While this account overstates the party's role, when Local 890 was Red-baited by the mining companies, the press, and the steelworkers' union—which was anxious to take over the local—its members rose to defend their leadership, Communist and non-Communist alike, respecting its judgment and trusting its decisions.

New Jersey Zinc, Empire's parent company, started to feel the losses from its New Mexico subsidiary. A last-ditch attempt at intimidation—repossessing furniture from a shop steward and another striker who lived in company housing—proved unsuccessful.

January 1952. Empire agreed to negotiations, and after nearly 15 months, the walkout ended with a new contract. Hot running water for company housing was not in the final settlement, but that luxury for the Mexican community came soon after. To celebrate their victory, one which hinted at racial and sexual equality, the brothers of Local 890 threw a banquet honoring the Ladies' Auxiliary and imported an *orquesta* from El Paso for the occasion.

Explaining his role in the Empire Zinc strike, Juan Chacón began in matter-of-fact tones, then warmed to the drama. His diffidence surrendered to intensity, and by the time the miners' wives squared off against the company thugs, he had transported himself back to mid-strike and was helping to map the next day's strategy.

~

The retelling of Local 890's fight against Empire Zinc might well have been limited to aging veterans of the struggle and footnotes in labor textbooks had not Paul Jarrico stumbled across the story during a visit to northern New Mexico. There on the San Cristobal ranch of Jenny and Craig Vincent, hosts to many McCarthy-era progressives in need of respite, Jarrico met Clint Jencks, who described the strike. Jarrico, a blacklisted Hollywood screenwriter and producer—his credits included Song of Russia and movies with Peter Lorre and Abbott & Costello—had recently formed an independent production company to develop progressive movies. Back in Los Angeles he described the events then unfolding in Grant County to his partners Michael Wilson, a screenwriter who had just won an Academy Award for *A Place in the Sun,* and Herbert Biberman, the director. Jarrico and Wilson were unemployable in Hollywood for refusing to testify before the

House Committee on Un-American Activities. Biberman, identified by writer Budd Schulberg as a Communist, served six months in federal prison for refusing to discuss his political inclinations.

This was not to be a conventional movie, the three agreed. First, the International Union of Mine, Mill and Smelter Workers would be a partner; second, the local mining community would have equal say in the script; and third, it would be filmed on location in Grant County, where most of the roles of miners and their families would be played by miners and their families.

After a visit to New Mexico, Michael Wilson completed a draft of the script and submitted it to the mining community at the union hall in Bayard, ten miles east of Silver City. The miners' strike was becoming a movie; the title was *Salt of the Earth*.

Local 890 had little compunction criticizing Wilson's script. Frances Williams, a Communist Party organizer from Los Angeles, came to help with revisions—necessary, according to one unionist, because the screenplay had the liberal white union man (modeled on Clint Jencks) saving the Mexican masses.

Ramón Quintero, the married union leader in the script who initially opposes women taking over the picket line and gradually appreciates their role in a class struggle for equality, has an affair with the wife of a miner off fighting in Korea. This sort of activity was not uncommon, the miners acknowledged, but the scene must be deleted because it reinforced the stereotype of the Latin male as an unfaithful cocksman. Wilson reluctantly agreed to excise the affair. In another scene while people are dancing, some beer spills and Esperanza—Ramón Quintero's wife—wipes up the mess with her dress. "I objected to that," Lorenzo Torrez remembered, "because of the stereotype that Chicanos are dirty, and that they aren't smart enough to use a towel." Another sensitive scene involved Ramón getting drunk while his wife asserts her new independence. Altered slightly, that part remained.

Assembling a crew proved to be another problem. The International Alliance of Theatrical and Stage Employees—IATSE—refused to allow its members to work on *Salt of the Earth* because of the movie's politics. That Hollywood unions wouldn't let their members work on such a pro-union film was bitter irony. Recruiting by word-of-mouth, personal pleas, and secret meetings eventually produced a skeleton crew. Jules Schwerin, who worked at RKO-Pathe Studios, signed on as unit manager and assistant director. Irving Hentshel, one of Hollywood's best propmen, agreed to work on *Salt,* bringing with him carpenter Bob Ames, who had been thrown out of the propman's union for his radicalism. A few blacks worked on the *Salt* crew, normally unheard of because of IATSE's Jim Crow attitude. Local 890 furnished manpower for the semi-skilled trades.

"See over there?"—we were back at the Roos spread the next day, and Juan Chacón pointed to the hillside as he continued his story—"This is where most of the filming took place. The mine, the picket line, almost all of the outside scenes were shot here." The visit to the location was Chacón's first since the movie had been made. His eyes froze, only to be melted by a sign reading private property. "We better be careful," he warned mischievously. "Someone might say we're trespassing and I'll land in jail again."

Casting the picture brought on more difficulties than finding a crew. Screen Actors Guild president Ronald Reagan personified the climate in Hollywood; no aspiring actor hoping to impress studio moguls would dare sign on with a gaggle of renegade lefties. From the beginning, though, Will Geer had agreed to play the sheriff, a wizened man who carries out the wishes of New Jersey Zinc ("Delaware Zinc" in the picture) but admires the spunk and resourcefulness of the mining community. Two local brothers reluctantly agreed to play his snarling and dumb deputies.

Rosaura Revueltas, an actress from a highly cultured Mexican family, took the role of Esperanza Quintero, the film's narrator, whose personal dignity and political growth symbolizes the community's sense of struggle. When she and her husband first read the screenplay, she told me years later at her home in Cuernavaca, he warned her that the movie would be nothing but trouble. "Well," she replied, "if this is the last film I make, I will do it." In early 1953 the English-speaking actress flew from Mexico City to Ciudad Juárez, crossed the border to El Paso where a U.S. immigration officer perfunctorily inspected her papers, and headed into Silver City.

All the major roles had been cast except Ramón Quintero, the male lead. Some professionals were considered along with a handful of miners. Rosaura Revueltas and others sat in on the readings and recommended one of the miners: 31-year-old Juan Chacón, whose union activities had expanded to Local 890's recording secretary and, finally, president. Biberman was skeptical; he thought Chacón much too shy, too small in stature, too sweet and retiring.

The first day of principal shooting was approaching, however, and with misgivings Biberman handed Chacón the script and told him to go up into the mountains and speak his lines to the rocks. Production began the day Dwight Eisenhower assumed the presidency from Harry Truman.

January 1953. Shooting began. A committee from the community and professional crew arranged for food, transportation, and baby-sitting. The Roos land proved ideal for outdoor scenes; the Fierro, a local nightclub, served well as the indoor sound stage. With a sizable deposit in the local bank, the Hollywood company was courteously received in small-town New Mexico. A local priest urged area merchants to rent automobiles, furniture, and other goods at low cost in exchange for God's blessings. "Those sonsabitches," the priest muttered to unit manager Schwerin after leaving the shops. "They hate the Mexican-Americans. Let them make some sacrifices."

Sheriff Goforth, who had handily won the Mexican vote the previous election, also cooperated. Late one night he took propman Hentshel into his office and, with the lights low, produced submachine guns and rifles to use as models in the propman's workshop. Juan Chacón surprised and pleased Biberman with his captivating portrayal. Other local residents gave similarly impressive performances, each drawing from a lifetime in the mining camps.

February 1953. Press attacks started. First, *The Hollywood Reporter:* "H'wood Reds are shooting a feature length anti-American racial issue propaganda movie." Then syndicated labor columnist Victor Reisel complained about the movie "not too far from the Los Alamos Atomic proving ground" in which "Tovarisch Paul [Jarrico] brought two carloads of Negroes into the mining town" for a scene involving mob violence against them. (That Silver City is 330 miles from the atomic proving grounds, and that no blacks appear in the picture, mattered little.) *Newsweek* headlined its article, "Reds in the Desert." Pathe, the Hollywood film developers, refused to process any more footage from *Salt*.

The next assault wave came from politicians. On Monday, February 24, on the floor of the U.S. House of Representatives, California Congressman Donald Jackson declared: "This picture is deliberately designed to inflame racial hatreds and to depict the United States of America as the enemy of all colored people." If shown in Latin America, Asia, and India, Jackson continued, "it will do incalculable harm...to the cause of free people everywhere." Jackson pledged "to do everything in my power to prevent the showing of this Communist-made film in the theaters of America." He asked Hollywood unions, studio executives, and the Departments of State, Commerce, and Justice how to prevent the film from being screened at home and abroad. Replied Howard Hughes of RKO: "If the motion picture industry—not only in Hollywood, but throughout the United States—will refuse these skills (processing, soundtrack, dubbing, editing facilities, etc.), the picture cannot be completed in this country."

Local ambivalence turned to antagonism; merchants stopped trading with the film company publicly (but welcomed its back-door business), the local theater suddenly refused to allow screenings of completed footage, and the priest suggested further telephone communication with the crew be carried out with code words. Immigration and Naturalization officials came to the Bear Mountain Lodge, where most of the professional cast and crew were staying, and lifted Rosaura Revueltas's passport, then returned a few days later to arrest her and take her to El Paso. During the 150-mile drive she was constantly asked, "Are you a Communist?" "Are your friends Communists?" In El Paso she was kept under armed guard in a hotel room. (Decades later, staying at Bear Mountain Lodge myself, I asked the owner about the film made by her celebrated guests. "That pink movie?" she replied derisively.)

The movie industry and the federal government were both trying to sabotage the film, the town was turning against it, and its leading lady had been spirited away. At the beginning of March the dam burst: Shots were fired at Clint Jencks's car, and an armed mob stormed filming in front of the union hall at Bayard, tossing down a camera and breaking it. "Shoot, you cowardly sonsabitches," Chacón dared, sticking out his chin. Someone grabbed Jencks and slapped him around; others were punched and shoved to the ground. Vigilantes met at a nearby American Legion Hall and declared open season on the crew: "Get out of Grant County or go out in black boxes." The governor and the state police attempted to neutralize the situation.

The Continental Divide cuts into Grant County in the shape of a snapping whip. Water flows east from there and water flows west from there, but water never flows across it. Much the same could be said for the attitudes festering there for years, so the crew stayed on. One scene necessitating Rosaura was shot with a stand-in, her back to the camera. Conditions deteriorated with helicopters overhead, stray gun shots whizzing by, stink bombs, tapped telephones, and opened (and resealed) mail. Out-of-town goons arrived to join the attacks; the crew hurriedly completed filming the bare necessities and left town. An Anglo union member's home was burned to the ground, and the Mine-Mill union hall at Carlsbad, 320 miles east, also burned down. An attempt to burn Local 890's building was unsuccessful. *The El Paso Herald-Post* congratulated the vigilantes "in their determination to clear away the pink overcast from their beautiful country."

The government conceded that the error in Rosaura's passport was theirs, but the admission came too late. Front-page stories in Mexico complained about the scandalous treatment of one of their own. "This is a contemptible insult to every Mexican citizen," declared Diego Rivera. In the movie's final scene, Rosaura stands alone, bursting with pride at what has been accomplished, the mountains of Grant County etched in the background. Actually they are mountains south of Mexico City, where her last scene was filmed shortly after she returned home. Likewise her narration, which provides the continuity of the film and the evolution of the women, was taped in Mexico and brought into the States under the guise of audition tapes from an unknown actress.

Editing and cutting were carried out clandestinely throughout Southern California. Actor Will Geer made his Topanga Canyon ranch available for much of the work. Musicians recording the soundtrack were told they were providing background music for a travelog, *Vaya con Dios*. Film was processed at different laboratories, submitted under false names. Despite all these hardships, by the beginning of 1954 *Salt of the Earth* was complete.

The film never achieved general release. Theaters agreed to run the movie, then buckled under to pressure from Hollywood executives, the projectionists' union, or local American Legionnaires to drop it. Movie houses in New York, Los Angeles, and San Francisco briefly resisted the blacklist. Reviews, though spotty, were generally favorable: "Wilson's tautly muscled script develops considerable personal drama," said the *New York Times*. The *San Francisco Chronicle*: "The film pulsates with a feeling of actuality." *The Los Angeles Times,* however, called the story "a diatribe," in which the Mexicans were "alleged victims of discrimination." When the Sky-Vue Drive-In near Silver City premiered *Salt,* cars were lined up for miles, it seemed, and the run, originally scheduled for a few days, lasted three weeks. Rosaura Revueltas earned national acclaim at home following the Mexico City opening of *La sal de la tierra.*

The tendency in assessing *Salt of the Earth* generations later is to magnify its content and effect, yet part of its appeal lies in its durability. "It's the only film I've ever worked on," Paul Jarrico told me, "that got better over the years instead of worse." The mining camp is frozen in time, but the powerful portrayal of human dignity and social realism is timeless. Equality for women and Mexican-Americans entwines with collective bargaining, each drawing strength from the other. Despite efforts to bludgeon it to death, *Salt of the*

Earth became an underground classic, the source of a number of books, and at least one documentary whose title draws on what the blacklisted cineasts committed: *A Crime to Fit the Punishment*. An opera called *Esperanza,* based on the movie, had its world premiere in 2000. And in Grant County, New Mexico, miners no longer take zinc from the land where the original *Salt* strike took place. Many of the underground shafts are flooded and the concentrator has since been demolished. In 1998 the Phelps Dodge Company purchased the remains of the old Empire Zinc facility.

In reviewing the strike and subsequent movie it is easy to confuse the two, such is the overlap of forces at play and people at work. Was the Grant County sheriff really a softy, or was that just Will Geer? Did the Empire Zinc executives watch the goings-on from afar or were those Delaware Zinc actors? To further confuse matters, Juan and Virginia Chacón had a baby girl during the filming and named her Esperanza after the leading role. Baby Esperanza had a crawl-on role in the movie as Juanito, Ramón and Esperanza Quintero's baby boy. When the real Esperanza grew up, she worked as a secretary at Local 890 for her father and other unionists.

In looking over my interviews with the principals in the strike and the film, I had to make sure the two piles didn't get mixed up. The strike and the movie blur; one defines the other. Finally, in sly homage to the film, director John Sayles took a memorable jailhouse line from *Salt* and inserted it in his early low-budget classic, *Return of the Secaucus Seven*. In the crowded lockup, Esperanza needs to feed her baby. "We want the formula!" her compañeras chant, to draw the sheriff's attention. "We want the formula!" When Sayles's characters are mistakenly detained for killing a deer, they break into the same chant at the police station, then burst out laughing. Both inside and outside the film industry, a healthy respect for the film endures.

Blacklisted filmmakers Michael Wilson and Paul Jarrico moved to France in 1958. Wilson returned in the mid-1960s and continued to write screenplays until his death in 1978. "The picture has international impact," he told me at his home in Ojai, California a few years earlier, "the power of which one cannot estimate in any tangible way." His only regret was having allowed realistic portions of his script to be tampered with for political reasons.

Paul Jarrico, who moved back and forth between France and the States before returning permanently, remained active in films until his death in 1997. "At the time of *Salt,*" he offered, "I thought it was too black-and-white, too polemical, too ideological. But now I feel that one of the reasons that people react so well is that *Salt* says that labor and minorities and women are all right in fighting for equality."

Unit manager Jules Schwerin, who lives in New York, also remained in the industry. "Filmmaking is a tough enough craft without loading it with political struggles," he told students at college screenings of *Salt*. Although he chose not to attach his name to the movie's credits when it first came out, many years later he lamented, "There are still people who were on the crew who do not wish to identify themselves with *Salt of the Earth.*"

Bob Ames, the assistant propman, became so enamored of the Grant County mining community that he returned to paint murals on their union hall.

Union organizer Clint Jencks was eased out of Mine-Mill in 1956 during his lengthy and ultimately victorious battle with the U.S. government over his alleged Communist Party affiliation. He stayed in touch with the southwestern New Mexico mining community during his long tenure teaching economics in southern California.

Rosaura Revueltas, as she feared, was blacklisted by the Mexican film industry after *Salt of the Earth*. She remained active in theater, though, working on the stage in East Berlin and Havana, eventually settling in Cuernavaca. The entranceway to her home was lined with gifts from 20th-century Latin American luminaries such as Diego Rivera and Pablo Neruda. She had aged gracefully, retaining the intensity and spark that made her performance in the movie so commanding.

"Everyone tells me I should be rich from the picture. But I never made a cent. Never."

Revueltas supported herself by teaching hatha yoga in a garage studio next to her swimming pool. Invited to attend a 1982 reunion of strikers and filmmakers in Silver City for the premiere of *A Crime to Fit the Punishment,* she was treated harshly at the American Embassy in Mexico City when she applied for a visa, then delayed at the border while the INS checked her old files. Lingering community resentment of the Mexican star in their midst from 30 years earlier surfaced at the reunion. "I had to endure the tasteless scenes of jealousy," she wrote me afterward. "Definitely they never liked me. But what makes me most unhappy is that *Salt of the Earth* is still alive, not because it is an excellent work of art but because the problems it deals with are the same after decades. Nothing has really changed. Too bad, too bad." Revueltas died in 1996.

Juan Chacón was reelected president of Local 890 regularly until 1963, when he was defeated and returned to work for Kennecott. Ten years later he ran for the presidency again, and won. Thirty years after taking part in one of the most militant strikes of the last few generations and the film it inspired, Chacón still presided over Local 890. His vision remained the same as the morning he was told, "All we have for Mexicans is labor."

Copies of *People's World* and *Family Circle* lay on the dining table of his house next to the apple orchard. Jesus Christ on black velvet hung above the living-room fireplace. A German poster advertising *Salz der Erde* hung on the opposite wall. Although his formal education ended after eight years, Chacón was a well-read man with a bookshelf full of provocative literature.

"I've been reading up on environmental matters," he volunteered in the apple orchard one afternoon. "The smog problem goes back to the 1800s in England. Virginia and I went to an environmental hearing in Silver City about Kennecott's new smelter, and people who have worked for them for years spoke in favor of allowing lax standards."

Virginia joined us. "If you drive between Bayard and Hurley and your window is down," she said, "your throat burns. That's the way the community has grown. They don't want to learn. Their concern is solely economic. Some people have died of heart attacks brought on by the fumes."

"There's still some discrimination against Mexican miners," Chacón acknowledged. "There always will be. The houses we lived in back then were awful. The Mexican people had two rooms—a kitchen and a bedroom. People don't believe it, but it was so! The movie had a big bearing on that. And the idea of allowing minorities to work with the Anglos. People got ideas from the movie and the strike."

We went back inside. Virginia herself had devoted decades to the union cause, but her attitude about the film was less cheery and more chary. "The movie didn't make any big difference. A lot of the women are still very much oppressed by the men, I'm sorry to say. That's the way it was and that's the way it's going to be. It didn't change my life. You can't teach an old dog new tricks."

Mine-Mill finally voted itself out of existence in 1966; 890 was among the last of the locals to switch over to the United Steel Workers of America. "We used to have the president and vice-president of Mine-Mill come and give strong talks to the men. The Steel Worker heads don't do that," Chacón lamented. "The labor movement is weak all over now, and union leaders have a weaker attitude toward the companies. They even try to settle contract negotiations without a strike."

The tedium of his job—grievance hearings, contract negotiations, membership recruitment, safety reviews, insurance forms, disability claims—these things did not deflate him. Reviewing contract proposals for yet another round of labor-management bargaining,

Juan entertained his union brothers by mimicking an exasperated company negotiator's paternalistic pleading: "Now, Mr. Chacooooone. You know we can't meet these demands of yours…"

The retired Mine-Mill charter still hung in Local 890's meeting room: "Labor Produces Wealth," it said. "Wealth Belongs to the Producers Thereof."

"Well, it's a constant struggle," Chacón said with a grin when the slogan was pointed out to him. "I guess I was born to be this way—mess around with people, help them if I can. I love it."

Not long after the *Salt* reunion to celebrate the union struggle and the Hollywood film, Chacón moved south to Deming, New Mexico, to be by himself. He died of self-imposed loneliness in 1985. The funeral service attracted workers from throughout the Southwest to celebrate an adventurous working-class hero from another era.

The film *Salt of the Earth,* the union struggle that inspired it, and the book and film *Milagro Beanfield War* have become part of the landscape of the American Southwest; they live in that neighborhood on the far side of the interstate, running through arroyos just beyond the distant mountain ranges. When we finally demand visas for visitors entering this quadrant of the country from the east, north, and west, as we do from the south, you'll be asked to take a cultural literacy test. *Salt of the Earth* and *Milagro Beanfield War* will be on it.

Start studying.

DEATH BY MISADVENTURE

Raising roosters to kill each other is repulsive and repugnant. To us. To bet on roosters as you might a horse at the Preakness or your alma mater in the NCAA basketball finals bewilders most of us. I've gone to cockfights a few times here and in Mexico, and the difference between them is like the difference between...the United States and Mexico. At a new cockfight arena in Sonora, Mexico, mariachis, civic boosters, and local personalities celebrate as if inaugurating a fancy major league stadium. Go to a cockpit in the States and snarly security lugheads eye you suspiciously as you drive into the parking lot.

In the last year of the last century cockfighting finally became illegal in Arizona. The action, a citizen's initiative on the ballot, left Louisiana, Oklahoma, and parts of rural New Mexico as the only places where you can still watch legal cockfighting. Damn shame, too, said Belton Hodges, a lifelong cockfighter. I met Hodges through the late Kemper Marley, the Arizona liquor dealer implicated—but never indicted—on a number of crimes, including the murder of an investigative reporter in Phoenix. Marley was a lifelong cockfighter, and I had written him to request an interview on cockfighting. He wrote back suggesting I speak with Hodges. "I was instructed to talk with you," Hodges said over the phone. "Tell you everything you want to know."

We met early one morning over huevos rancheros at a South Phoenix diner. "My father was in cockfighting," said Belton Hodges. "My grandfather, too. We've been treated roughly by reporters. We've been set up and shown in the poorest light *(spit)*. You hunt?"

I shook my head.

"But you do chew a toothpick, I see. Watch out, the tree-huggers'll getcha."

Hodges, who turned 79 the same year that his beloved cock-fighting became illegal in Arizona, punctuated his observations by spitting a cheek full of Red Man into an empty Rolaids bottle, a practice he repeated with precision every 90 seconds.

"We're not rabid. We simply have a real strong competitive desire. Eighty-five percent of our people are ex-servicemen *(spit)*. Some of us are lawyers. There's a place for the Humane Society, but they're out to change our whole lifestyle from a meat-eating society to all vegetarians. They categorize us as dope peddlers and illiterates. We're accused of being cruel, vicious, barbaric, bloodthirsty, prehistoric, and Neanderthal. I've never been arrested. My wife and daughter have never been prostitutes. Courage and bravery are not revered anymore. They're frowned on *(spit)*."

My own first cockfight experience in the Southwest took place in Avondale, west of Phoenix. This was a number of years ago, when animal-rights activists made their annual stink about how the state legislature spinelessly caved in to the cockfight lobby. One weekday afternoon I borrowed a friend's big old white Caddy and motored out to the Copper State Game Club, run by a fellow named Doyle Thompson. When I turned south off the highway into the grounds, the place was empty, and I walked around quietly absorbing the atmosphere. Hundreds of wooden seats surrounded a center stage where roosters would thrash it out in matches that had already been attacked in the press. The place was clean, even antiseptically so, with no hint of sleazy bettors or fowl carnage. Suddenly a large, lean, stupid-looking fellow appeared and menacingly asked what I was doing. He wore a dirty T-shirt, blue jeans, and work boots. He appeared to be in his late 20s.

I've been to cockfights in Mexico, I explained, and I simply wanted to see what the difference was north of the border. "I'm a writer," I foolishly added. I might just as well have said I smite first-born Christians.

The galoot broke into a slow, savage grin. Did anyone know I was here? No, I innocently told him, it was more a spur-of-the-moment trip. His smile grew wider and more brutish as he motioned toward a drainage ditch. "Then no one will know where to look for you if you turn up missing, will they." This he said more as a statement than a question, and my adrenaline started pumping.

"No one except my wife and my editor, that is."

The doofus didn't know I had neither at the time, but the possibility of either was enough to bring our encounter to a rocky but conversational close. He escorted me back to the Caddy and I drove away.

Too bad, too, because I had wanted to meet Thompson, who stood to gain the most from the cockfights and lose the most if they were banned. I had to wait a few years until Doyle moved his operation to the banks of the Colorado River in Ehrenberg, Arizona, across from Blythe, California.

That's where I paid a $12 entrance fee and strolled into the new Copper State Game Club. Beneath its yellow-and-white-striped circus tent, the smell of fresh paint and chicken shit dominated. Hundreds of metal, wooden, and cushioned seats faced the dirt center stage, which had a white chalk line down its center. It may have been "the Hilton of Game Clubs," as advertisements claimed, but if that was true I'd hate to see the Motel 6 version.

I finally tracked down Doyle Thompson for a primer on his sport. I flashed my newly acquired Arizona Game Breeders Association membership card, and we started talking. He looked like a young Warren Beatty.

"Beginners like the long-knife tournaments," Thompson explained during the weigh-in. "One-two-three and it's over. You go through a lot of birds in a day." He was describing the stab-stab matches, but most of Copper State's matches were of the slice-slice flavor. Just as I reached my seat, a scratchy recording of the "Star Spangled Banner" erupted over the PA system. I placed my cap over my heart and joined the audience of several hundred as it stood and faced the Stars and Stripes.

About the cap: It's navy blue and shows two roosters flailing at each other. I paid six dollars for it at the concession stand in a silly attempt to blend in. They also sold books on cockfighting, velvet art, videos, and back copies of *Gamecock,* a monthly that began publication before World War II. Its articles, geared for the cock breeder, describe in clinical detail how to improve your brood, strengthen your birds, and maintain them in the pink of health. Its advertisements sold pills, ointments, equipment for raising birds, and veterinary equipment for treating them.

The crowd came from all over the West, especially Bakersfield and Phoenix. Two fellows the spittin' image of the Bartles and Jaymes wine cooler duo flew in from Kentucky for the weekend match. The retired pair liked what they saw. "We've been to some of the other major pits—Biloxi and Orlando—but you've got the best cockfights in the country here in Arizona," Bartles said slowly. "You've also got the best-looking birds here," Jaymes added even slower, "and the healthiest red faces, too. They've got good feathers and they're well cared for." It was, I think, the oddest compliment ever paid Arizona.

I know I shouldn't like cockfights. I've been to bullfights twice, big elaborate affairs with terrific decorum and ceremonial splendor, admirable clothes and grand tradition. On both occasions I left at halftime; I couldn't even fake enjoying them. Man fights beast: The odds are stacked against the latter, and the crowd roots for the former. Unlike bullfights, though, cockfights don't leave me cold. Of course they're disgusting, but it's violence on a less-than-human scale. Cheerfully tolerating cockfights runs counter to everything civil I like to think I identify with. Still, the fact is that I've enjoyed the tackiness of the half-dozen cockfights I've attended in the United States and Mexico: the cigarette-strewn rubble, the pre-match betting, the slice (so to speak) of life—even, occasionally, the birds going at each other. Certainly it's a cringe-worthy scene toward the end when one rooster mercilessly pierces the other with its steel spurs, but it's nothing more than dumb bird versus dumber bird. I was a conscientious objector during the war against Vietnam, but my draft board never asked me about help-less roosters.

The first fight at the game club along the Colorado began with Mike squaring off against Buck. Both men delicately cradled their birds as they approached the midpoint of the pit. They fit no blood-thirsty stereotype; they looked more like neighborhood grease monkeys. The two rocked back and forth in an almost sexual rhythm as their birds pecked at each other in a ritual called billing. In its own way, the affection the handlers showed for their roost-ers was touching, even tender. Thinking back to their demeanor, I am reminded of the sad and determined Carlos Zaragoza, the protagonist in Tom Russell's terrific borderland ballad, "Gallo del Cielo" ("Rooster from Heaven").

Then the referee—what a job!—signaled the fight to begin. Mike and Buck kissed their birds, whispered to them softly, and placed them on the ground. The two roosters went at each other, wings waving madly, steel spurs flailing and feathers flying. The cocks' natural spurs had been cut away, replaced with long, curved metal blades carefully tied on their legs. Knife-like gaffs are used for stab-stab competitions; other derbies restrict the sharpness of the gaffs to their points only. Both varieties could be purchased from the vendor who sold me my cap.

The audience sounded like an apiary a block away, and bettors looked around for each other. Betting heats up in the opening minutes of a match, when both birds strut their stuff but neither has a distinct advantage. I caught the attention of a man in an open red flannel shirt two sections away; through a series of nods, gestures, and lip-reading, I took Buck and he took Mike. Buck seemed a sympathetic character. Ten dollars. No odds. The program said, "HONESTY AND FAIR PLAY/WE WILL MAKE NO EXCEPTIONS."

Except for the initial flurry, the first few minutes were as dull as a Floyd Patterson-Ingemar Johansson fight. For all the interest the two birds took in each other, they could have been doing their nails. Then, almost by accident, Mike's bird suddenly plunged into Buck's, and their wings and legs got all tangled up a few feet above the ground. When they landed, still clutching one another, the referee called "Handle!" Each handler picked up his bird to massage its wings, sponge off its beak, and in Buck's case to wipe away the blood pulsing from its punctured gullet. That's not a pretty sight, but for the Copper State crowd it was all in a day's play.

As an interested third party, I can report the following: After the first handle break, the two fowl faced off again and tangled once more. Buck's bird, a bit debilitated from the first round, was slower to respond, a weakness that Mike's cock exploited to full advantage. Like a losing prizefighter on the ropes, Buck's rooster clutched his stronger opponent, preventing him from inflicting more damage. Handle after handle dragged the fight out, extending the agony of death for the chickens—and the payoffs for the bettors. The crowd grew noisily impatient. When Buck's bird could move no more—

blood was choking its beak, oozing from its wounds, and splattering the white sideboards—it finally lay on its side. Daid.

Buck tried to nurse his bird back to life, but its head hung like a plumb bob. He repeatedly lifted it up; each time, it flopped back down again. A coroner's report would have identified the cause of death as "multiple puncture wounds."

For a couple of seconds, the silence was deader than Buck's bird—whether in tribute to the fallen rooster or for winners and losers to calculate the money about to change hands, I couldn't tell. Buck, wearing a wan smile, picked up his bird by the tail feathers and walked off-pit, blood still dripping from the late rooster's neck. "What's eating me is not that I think roosters have souls," said a friend who accompanied me to Ehrenberg, "but that humans should have more heart than this." Losers like Buck's were carted away in a wheelbarrow to a nearby landfill for burial next to paper cups from Wendy's and plastic bags from 7-Eleven, and I sheepishly handed two fives to the man in the red flannel shirt.

Mexican cockfights are livelier, bloodier, and more musical. Between each fight, singers take center stage. Neighbors trade backslaps and laugh at family jokes. The birds come from farther away; some even bring their own cheering sections. Respect trumps suspicion, camaraderie beats mistrust. In both countries, though, after everyone else has gone home, a lonely man with a wide push broom stays all night.

"Colonel Sanders keeps his chickens shoulder-to-shoulder indoors, and in six weeks they're slaughtered." Belton Hodges again. "Ours are far better cared for. They get a lot of fresh air." One night before leaving for Ehrenberg, a friend and I had discussed cockfights over a Chinese dinner. When the fortune cookies came, mine said "BIRDS ARE ENTANGLED BY THEIR FEET AND MEN BY THEIR TONGUES." That message came back to me as Belton continued. "You know *(spit)*, cockfighting is probably the oldest spectator sport known to mankind. Guys would go through the jungle, see gamecocks fighting, and stop to enjoy it. Thomas Jefferson had fighting cocks. Lincoln was a referee at a match. Will Rogers knocked Fatty Arbuckle on his ass betting on a cockfight *(spit)*. There's been an influx of Latinos into cockfighting. Hot-blooded bastards. They brought drinking to cockfighting, and even some dope."

Belton drove me over to Henry's place. Henry ran an industrial-strength cock-breeding ranch in Phoenix—300 gamecocks in various stages of preparation for the half-dozen fights of their lives. They looked in the best of health under the finest of care. If they retired undefeated—that is to say, alive—they would each be rewarded with a lifetime boudoir of hens.

"They're fed and watered twice a day *(spit)*. I've been at it all my life. My chickens cost me $2,000 a year, but I've never made any money. The people who make the money are the feed, medicine, and equipment guys. We took a survey of our members. Most keep their chickens in an 8-by-6-foot pen that costs $150. Each bird gets vaccinated *(spit)*. Then there are booster shots, vet costs, the property itself, and construction material. We pump a lot of money into the state's economy."

Here at Henry's place, in a cleanly mowed field next to the brood-cock pen, hundreds of chickens were tethered to their own private coops. We were about to open a gate leading to the field when a nasty dog sprang up and started barking. "I'm not going in there with that damn Rottweiler," Belton muttered. "When Henry comes back I'll have him lock him up *(spit-spit)."*

Henry put a slight nick in the web of each chicken's feet to identify it. Thanks to his elaborate records, he knew the age, lineage, breed, and fight records of each fowl. When Henry finally joined us, he confessed he hadn't liked cockfighting at first sight. "It took me two years to understand it," he said. Finally, Henry was converted; now he lived for his roosters, and his roosters did the same—and more—for him. He was the cock of the walk.

At last Belton took me to his own spread, where he devoted an entire house to cockfighting. A porcelain rooster sat below the bathroom mirror. A wooden cock hung on the wall. Most walls bore paintings of fighting roosters. Behind the house lay cage after cage of well-groomed roosters nearing fight status. A radio played a Phoenix "lite rock" station's repertoire of Billy Joel, Carly Simon, and others all day. "It pacifies them," he assured me, and on this point alone I believed him totally. With Elton John serenading his chickens, I asked Belton if he ever saw the famously reclusive Kemper Marley. In tribute to his years in the cockfight world, Marley had been the guest of honor at the Ehrenberg arena the weekend I visited.

"He has some of the best fighting chickens in the country," Hodges said, "but we don't slop out of the same trough. His is platinum; mine's timber. My class of people, we're in it for the sport *(spit)*. In the old days we'd sit on bales of hay and watch. The whole family'd come. It was a picnic."

Belton Hodges was the cockfight industry's de facto spokesman against the state-ballot initiative, which eventually put his hobby out of business by a margin of 2 to 1. You didn't need sophisticated demographics, though, to know that at the close of the 20th century the Southwest's mobility made Winnebagos and frequent-flier miles more common than steel gaffs and backyard cockfights. Even rural sheriffs endorsed the initiative, acknowledging that drugs and drunkenness had become part of the matches.

One by one, the mom-and-pop cock-breeding enterprises in the state's rural south took down their roadside signs. The promoters left the state. Doyle Thompson, they say, moved to Louisiana. And by the time I left his Colorado River cockfight arena, I had lost more money in a single day than I had pledged to my public radio station all year.

∼

Movie sets and land swindlers, recreational vehicles and curious art, men at play with roosters at war—they all help shape our regional heritage. But nothing contributes more to Southwestern tradition than violence. We celebrate guns and bombs here, almost always in the wrong hands and for the wrong reasons.

I spent an afternoon in the late 1980s with a gun manufacturer in Phoenix who was touting his new prototype, the Piranha. He believed the Piranha incorporated the first genuinely new pistol technology since the early 1900s. Joe Smith, he said his name was. Smith produced a 9mm chunk of metal, removed the outer casing, and lay the gun on his desk. "See? Where the toggle used to go up, now it goes down. There's a spring under it now. This pistol has an 85 percent reduction in recoil. It's virtually free of any malfunction or breaking of its parts. I think it will dominate the market. Right now we're just struggling. We're just little people trying to put a gun business together. We worked for two years on the trigger alone." The rosewood handle made the Piranha a handsome pistol, and its accessories—a 16-inch carbine barrel, for one—gave it the range and accuracy shooters want.

Smith described his market. "First, gun nuts—people who buy guns because they're different. Then there are the collectors, because they have to have it. The third group is the ones who'll go out and shoot them. Homeowners. For self-defense. Especially females. We have a semi-automatic .380 for them. The frame fits a woman's hand. It weighs 2.7 pounds." He handed it to me to test its heft. Smith's last target group included people who shoot at varmints, state road signs, and natural monuments.

"This is the safest weapon in existence." Smith was so proud of the Piranha, he could hardly contain himself. "We plugged up a barrel with mud and it shot smoothly. Let's say you parachute behind enemy lines." I tried real hard to imagine parachuting behind enemy lines, but the closest I could come was parasailing along the coast at Puerto Vallarta. "If everyone else shot at you with a conventional pistol, you'd have all the advantages. Since it has no recoil, cops don't have to take the time to recover from the first shot to take the second, and crooks won't have a chance to put a bullet in them."

We strolled over to the Piranha target-practice area. Smith fired a few rounds at a sheet of brown paper mounted on a large foam backing 20 feet away. His arm was steady, his eyes stayed open, and his aim was true. Three of his five shots hit within inches of dead center. He handed the Piranha prototype to me and motioned to the target.

"I don't think this is a good idea," I said. "I haven't fired a weapon in years."

Actually, the last gun I'd fired had been in a video arcade years earlier. I've managed to live my entire life with no desire or interest in owning or shooting a weapon, and I don't expect that to change. Once in the mid-1970s I was working on a particularly grisly story and an off-duty federal agent offered to take me out to the scene of the crime, located on private property. "Better carry this," he said, handing me a small pistol. "Put it in your pocket. Can't tell who we'll run into." My hesitancy brought scorn from the fed. "What are you afraid of?"

That question surfaced in my mind as Smith handed me his Piranha. Simply shooting at an indoor target wouldn't be so terrible. "Okay," I said, and faced the mounted brown paper. The gun felt light to my touch, and with a ten-inch barrel and no mounted sight, well, how could I miss? I held my arm straight out, aimed, squinted my eyes like I'd seen in the movies, and fired.

As Smith had advertised, the recoil I'd braced my body for was barely perceptible. I fired again. And again. After the last round, Smith and I walked over to the target. No holes in the brown paper. No holes in the foam backing. In fact, we couldn't find the shells anywhere. Smith politely excused my disastrous showing, explaining that my preparation for a recoil worked against me. We went back to his office, where he cleaned the gun and stripped it down.

A decade earlier, I did come perilously close to firing a weapon. I was working a story about Mike Bowan, a fast-draw expert who lived in Casa Grande, between Phoenix and Tucson. Bowan had entered his first fast-draw competition in Tombstone, Arizona, just three years earlier and had become a fixture at Southwest tournaments. He explained the subtleties of his sport to me at his home, then took me out into the desert for a demonstration. He shot faster than a camera shutter and punched holes in Coors cans—his can of preference—with exceptional accuracy.

Willing to lose my shooter's virginity, I took a turn. Bowan instructed me in great detail how to coordinate my body's movement with my hand's action. But as he strapped his holster over my hips, the fatal flaw surfaced: His rig was for right-handed shooters and I'm left-handed. "Well," he assured me, "it's easy to shoot. It's Western. I think more people are going back to the old style of living. To Western living. Why, if I didn't live in a trailer park, I could practice in my own backyard."

A couple of months later Cal Elrich told me that nothing wrecks your fast-draw more than a good night's sleep, and that accounted for the cement contractor's presence at the Hacienda Hotel black-jack tables at 3:30 in the morning. I'd gone to Las Vegas to write about a fast-draw contest and found Cal's gait in the "walk-and-draw" competition oddly appealing. He was built like Babe Ruth, with thin legs supporting a heavy torso. When he approached the shooter's line, he walked with catlike tread, daintily, on tiptoes. Pulling the gun from its holster, he jerked his body back and made a sudden grunting noise as if hoisting a 100-pound sack of cement. He won at blackjack and he won in the walk-and-draw.

The event attracted gamblers waking up from their previous night's losses. Blinking in the midday sun, most people passing by the parking lot assumed a television show was being filmed. The day's biggest draw was Bob Munden, "the fastest gun in the world." Munden's fast-draw ability rated him a line in the *Guinness Book of Records,* and his international notoriety gave him a soapbox to proclaim about global order. "The trend in Western movies is like the trend in all movies. It's the anti-violence thing. If the world was as violence-free as they'd like to have it, I think this place would be a little boring. There's a lot of people who are down on everything short of sitting in a rockin' chair. I don't know what the problem is. The trend of people—the way they're put together— seems to be changing." The wives of both Bob Munden and Mike Bowan, Rebecca and Hazel, also shot fast-draw.

Guns have been such a part of daily life in the Southwest that few were taken aback by a music company's display ad in the Tucson newspapers one day. "Free Shotgun with Any Piano or Organ," it promised. Pictured one atop the other was a rifle and a church organ.

This preoccupation of mine—writing about faux gunslingers and real gun manufacturers—was somewhat unsettling. I suppose it had to do with exploring the twists and turns of upbringing: What twist had sent them in one direction but turned me in another? Why were guns the first thing they thought of in the morning and of no concern to me all day?

I finally met my match in John Dane, a British mercenary living in Utah in the mid-1970s. Dane, who had served with U.S. forces in Vietnam, stole weapons from National Guard armories, ran paramilitary training camps for clandestine Mormon groups, smuggled weapons to Central America through Arizona, hired out as an assassin, and loved to play Bach on a church organ. I spent many months researching and interviewing him, in jail and in his mercenary lair along the San Rafael River near Cleveland, Utah. Though I found him a fascinating thug of the first order, I became nauseous from the violence that he and the others took for granted. I soon left them alone.

⁓

For Joe, the Piranha promoter, playing with guns was business. For fast-drawers Mike, Cal, and Bob, it was sport. For John the mercenary, guns were his bathrobe and slippers. And Domingo Sanchez considered a gun crucial to his job.

"Someone's going to get shot," Sanchez warned impassively after receiving a call on his two-way radio from the U.S. Border Patrol station at Chula Vista, California. We had been driving along a dirt road that divides Mexico from the United States when we saw a black car pause to pick up some people on the U.S. side about half a mile away. Sanchez took off in pursuit, caught up with the car, and motioned it over. As the driver handed Sanchez his ID, a second Border Patrol agent arrived. Then a passenger in the black car, instead of showing his ID, slowly produced a gun. Sanchez quickly pulled out his service revolver and aimed it square at the man's head. The less-experienced agent did the same; as his arms began to shake, he yelled at the armed passenger, "Put that gun down or I'll blow your fuckin' head off!" The fellow seemed bemused by the situation and held on to his weapon, twisting and turning it for a long five seconds. Finally he put it down.

Later, after the Mexicans who were the cause of the drama had been processed, Sanchez and two other agents talked about how close to bloodshed the predicament had come.

"You shoulda iced him, Mingo," said one. "You shoulda shot him."

"If you can get away with it, go ahead," offered the other.

"Yeah," Sanchez replied. "I shoulda shot him…no, I shouldn'ta."

Violence along the 2,000-mile border with Mexico takes many forms. Migrant Mexicans are prey to attacks from frustrated ranchers, from their fellow countrymen, and from trigger-talking Border Patrol agents. Yet the Border Patrol is neither the cause nor the solution to the troubles that plague the multitude of foreigners who cross America's lower boundary. In the Chula Vista incident, it turned out that the weapon in the black car had been an air gun—and an unloaded one at that. Still, the hint of violence hung in the air like spent gunpowder.

My day with Sanchez took place during the Carter years, when border violence was not yet routine. All the more reason, then, for the sad plight of Elfego Mendoza to gain such notoriety at the time. It was March 1976 when Mendoza and two cousins crossed into the States east of Sonoyta, Mexico, the town that leads to the Pinacate volcanic field. Mendoza had left Quaxilotla—their dirt-road village of 200 in the state of Guererro—a few days earlier and spent the night in Sonoyta on the floor of an abandoned house. He hoped to return home for the planting season a few months later.

An old, unused jeep trail heads north just inside the eastern boundary of Organ Pipe Cactus National Monument, and Mendoza and countless others found it an agreeable way to enter this strange country. The backcountry road gradually climbs to Sweetwater Pass, an east-west wilderness thoroughfare that leads between the Ajo Mountains and Díaz Peak. Sweetwater Pass, which follows an arroyo, has been popular with generations from the north for its challenging camping and with generations from the south for its convenience. Its eastern end comes out on a rough dirt road on the Tohono O'odham Indian Reservation, where contraband—human and otherwise—can be picked up and driven north to State Route 86 and beyond.

Had they been interested, Mendoza and his cousins would have appreciated the paloverde, the mesquite trees, and the desert shrub growing between the organ-pipe cactus and saguaro. They might have seen evidence of mule deer, coyotes, or javelinas. But when they got to Sweetwater Pass, the trio was ordered to halt; a border patrolman had detected their presence using a Vietnam-era infrared device called a body sensor.

Mendoza's cousins stopped, but Elfego ran. Double-ought buckshot pellets struck him in the neck, severing his spine. Elfego, then 25, woke up in the hospital to find himself a quadriplegic.

William Manypenny, the border patrolman who fired the crippling shot, told a version of events that changed from one report to the next. At first he said that he had found Mendoza lying paralyzed on the ground, and that the Mexican must have slipped. Then, acknowledging that his weapon had caused the wound, he said the buckshot must have ricocheted, or that he had slipped and the gun had gone off accidentally. Or he may have meant to fire a warning shot in front of Mendoza but misjudged his speed. Finally, Manypenny said he believed his partner had been in danger; he had fired in self-defense.

The Border Patrol dropped Manypenny—not for Mendoza's lifetime injury, but for carrying an unauthorized shotgun. Manypenny was found guilty of the shooting in federal court, but appeals on jurisdictional issues elevated the case all the way to the U.S. Supreme Court, where the ex-border patrolman lost. William Manypenny was eventually sentenced to 80 weekends in jail, plus three years of working with paralysis victims one day a week.

As for Mendoza, he recovered, sued the U.S. government, and was allowed to stay in Arizona, where his mother, his wife, and their three young children ultimately joined him. "I didn't know the dangers of coming to the United States," he told me in his new home in Phoenix. "Had I known, I wouldn't have come." It had been his first attempt at crossing the border. "I heard that what you can make in one month in Mexico, you can make in one week here."

"It was hard to see him go," said his wife, Adela, "but if he was to go, I wished him well. When I heard the bad news, that he had been shot, the days were like nights and the nights like days."

The Mendoza house was surrounded by concrete ramps to accommodate Elfego's wheelchair. His settlement with the government included a sizable trust fund to cover his lifelong medical expenses, plus enough to keep the family afloat for years to come. "We have more things here," Mrs. Mendoza acknowledged, "and we can pay for what we need. But it was better back in Mexico. Elfego was fine. We were poor, but we were all healthy."

Mendoza spent hours each day watching television shows beamed in from Mexico City, his only link at the time with his patria. "I miss my land in Mexico. I'd like to take a stroll down my street. I miss hearing the rooster crow when I'd get up early and go to work in the fields." He had no advice for others hoping to come to the United States. "Just let them look at me, that's all."

Elfego Mendoza still lives in the Phoenix area, and his three children have long since graduated from high school. Now, almost a quarter of a century after the incident, he understandably does not want to reflect on it.

But I do. More Manypennys have come and gone, and with them more Mendozas. Border violence has become routine. An acceptable level of madness permeates the frontier, a *locura* that has grown so commonplace we notice only its absence, not its presence. Rural, desolate Sweetwater Pass, meanwhile, has become such a heavily trafficked corridor that occasional volunteer cleanup brigades now venture through it, carting away truckloads of empty water bottles and other debris left by newly arrived overland immigrants.

~

We honor guns and commemorate bombs. Trinity Site, where the first atomic bomb was tested early one Monday morning in mid-July of 1945, opens its doors twice yearly for public visits. Until recently, visitors came by caravan from the K-Mart parking lot in Alamogordo, more than 200 miles south of Albuquerque, for the 90-minute drive through the White Sands Missile Range to Trinity Site. Today anyone can drive right up to the site itself on the visitor-designated Saturdays in the spring and fall. The possibility of getting radioactive dust on your fingers from Trinitite—the green, glassy substance brought into being by the explosion—was real enough that a sign warned visitors not to eat anything, put on makeup, or pick up objects from the ground. Pregnant women and small children were discouraged from attending. A stump of one leg of the detonation tower remains embedded in the earth a few feet from a lava-rock obelisk commemorating the event at Ground Zero.

Desert scrub has reclaimed much of the area known to Spanish explorers as La Jornada del Muerto, or Dead Man's Trail. When I traveled the jornada to Trinity Site in 1983, I met physicist Joe McKibben, who 38 years earlier had flipped one of the switches that set off the atomic age. "I started filming a panel meters in front of me for the record. Suddenly I became aware of the bomb—it illuminated the entire countryside." I peered closely at McKibben's fingers, but they looked no different from yours or mine.

Fifteen hundred visitors were at Trinity Site the day I dropped in, and we all saw the 400-foot-wide saucer-shaped cavity the explosion had carved in a gradual slope. The tourists included a 31-year-old radio engineer from El Paso, who carried a Geiger counter to measure radioactivity. "Against a normal background I would get about one count every five seconds," he explained to a few of us gathered around his makeshift research station. "Here I'm getting two or three counts every second."

A furniture salesman traveled to Trinity Site from Arkansas because "this is where the atomic age began." During his drive across Texas, he kept a journal of his thoughts about the atomic bomb and its significance. Forty peace demonstrators maintained a vigil at the gate, but I couldn't discern much difference of opinion between them and the rest of us. The Owl Bar in nearby San Antonio, New Mexico, does terrific business on visitors' day. Back in the 1940s, the bar regulars included physicists secretly working on the bomb.

It's too late for peace demonstrators to picket the 18 Titan II Intercontinental Ballistic Missile silos that surrounded Tucson from the mid-1960s to the mid-80s. The silo sites were supposedly top secret, but for those who drove southern Arizona's back highways, spotting the access roads to these ICBM hideaways was almost a game. Some locations were even common knowledge. If you took the Old Sonoita Highway off State Route 83 southeast of Tucson, for example, you'd come upon one. Another was secreted not far from the Green Valley retirement community off the highway to Nogales. When ICBMs were phased out and deactivated, the military converted the Green Valley silo into a visitor's center. In the mid-1990s, the Interior Department designated the Titan Missile

Museum a national historic landmark. International violence has no shortage of regional monuments.

~

My own monument to gratuitous violence is a house on Helen Street in Tucson near the University of Arizona. It's an unremarkable house, really, built from stucco and brick in the decade following World War I. The neighborhood near the university is filled with these roomy if occasionally down-at-the-heels homes. They were called California bungalows then, but now they're called student housing. In the spring of 1969, 18-year-old Dennis Murphey and some buddies lived in the house on Helen Street, neither full-time students nor fully employed. They lived outside the mainstream but not too far outside the law. Psychedelic drugs were a part of their lives, making them a harmless and inoffensive—if somewhat whacked-out—bunch.

Denny and his friends often ate at drive-ins, including the popular Johnie's Big Boy. Jean Elaine Palacios, also 18, had just landed a job there as a carhop. Jean, the eldest of eight children, lived with her family in Vandenberg Village, the residential area at Davis-Monthan Air Force Base, where her father was an aircraft mechanic. Master Sergeant Francisco Palacios had joined the Air Force in 1950, not long after graduating from high school in Puerto Rico. While on duty in Europe, he met and married a British woman. His children got their first exposure to America's new mores when Sergeant Palacios received orders to ship out stateside. The family moved to Arizona from England in mid-1968.

The owner of Johnie's warned Sergeant Palacios that Dennis Murphey, who started coming around often, would be nothing but trouble for the somewhat innocent Jean. He was right about one thing—she was attracted to Dennis. Around the beginning of May, she dropped out of high school and moved in with Denny at the Helen Street house. It was your basic hippie crash-pad with a permanent core, including Denny and a flow-through crowd of others who needed a place to stay now and then. With soft drugs and good music, the scene was little different from the one at many other houses around Tucson and the rest of the country. I never knew Murphey, but I must have sat on the hardwood floor of at least a dozen similar homes in town about that time.

The dope scene in Tucson was definitely getting more visible. By then, the city had become known throughout the country as a low-key port of entry for contraband from Mexico. Dealers would drive or fly into Old Pueblo, pick up their load, and be on their way. It was one of the only towns to sell peyote in the open, and one of the last to sell marijuana by the kilo. As late as 1962, however, Pima County had not yet logged a single drug-related prosecution. Eventually the county attorney's office planted a man in the barrio; his marijuana buys led to Tucson's first drug cases.

"Tucson was a very alive place then," recalls a musician from the era. "All the hipsters knew each other. The danger came from the airmen at Davis-Monthan. They'd beat the crap out of you in a Circle K parking lot if you had long hair. The police would just watch." Says another: "The place had a cowboy mentality. You could shoot your wife, but don't you dare kill someone's cow."

Still, there had been an active literary and music scene in town—poetic, experimental, just off the scope. Jack Kerouac's description held for many years: Tucson "was one big construction job," he wrote in *On the Road,* "the people transient, wild, ambitious, busy, gay; washlines, trailers; bustling downtown streets with banners; altogether very Californian." The area offered a bohemian sensibility. A community of artists took root on a spread north of town called Rancho Linda Vista, and musicians played at coffeehouses such as Portafino's, Sanders, and the Minus One.

The United Farm Workers grape boycott conferred a wholesome political identity on the town. The songs of internationally celebrated Tucson native Lalo Guererro gave the Mexican-American community emotional and clever lyrics about their barrio, their culture, and their identity. In Washington, Udall brothers Morris and Stewart presented a liberal face for Tucson. Activists got their anti-Vietnam War pamphlets at the Peace & Freedom Party storefront on Sixth Street. As the war grew simultaneously implacable and hopeless, adventurous Davis-Monthan airmen in civilian clothes dropped in to chat. KTKT, a local top-40 AM station, played progressive rock for a few hours late every night. It was a city that, like many others in America, reflected a counterculture growing amid a dominant community of orthodoxy that paid attention only when compelled.

Sergeant Francisco Palacios, then 46, was compelled. Distraught over his daughter's new life, he had assumed a strong paternal role—he did the grocery shopping, cooking, laundry, ironing, and house cleaning as well. He was beside himself when he learned that Jean had written a friend in England that she was smoking marijuana and couldn't wait to try LSD. Murphey was going to destroy his daughter, Palacios was convinced, and ruin her brain. Tormented, he asked friends on base what to do. Some offered to go tear Murphey's house apart. Desperate, he applied for a post in Vietnam that would allow him to take his daughter and his seven younger children away from the evil stateside influences.

The Grateful Dead had played on the University of Arizona campus shortly after Jean moved in with Denny, and the couple had almost certainly attended. Jean was starting to fit into the household routine. Then, one Saturday evening in late May, consumed by his daughter's situation, Sergeant Palacios rounded up a few of the family and drove across town to the house on Helen Street. When Jean came to the door, he ordered her to come home. It had been a particularly bad day for the 18-year-old: Earlier she had been arrested for shoplifting at Montgomery Ward. Jean went home with Daddy, leaving Denny in a quandary.

Denny decided to get Jean back that same night and telephoned the Palacios household after the family returned home around 11 p.m. The sergeant got on the line and challenged Dennis to come over right away; Jean grabbed the receiver from her father and yelled, "Don't come over here, Denny!"

He ignored her advice. He didn't have a car, but a fellow at the house offered to drive him to the base. Murphey, driver Gary Inman, and a few others piled into Inman's 1960 Ford convertible and headed east to Davis-Monthan. They were greeted by a big sign reading "PEACE IS OUR PROFESSION."

The guard at the main gate must have done a double take when Inman pulled up. Here were half a dozen youths of decidedly non-military bearing in a nine-year-old convertible missing both its top and its hood, its doors tied shut by rope. The sentry called the Palacios home, then gave the boys a visitors' pass and waved them on to Skyline Drive in Vandenberg Village.

Dennis told his friends to wait in the car and went up to the house. Sergeant Palacios answered the door. He saw a sullen fellow in sunglasses with long hair, a mustache, and a beard. "Are you Dennis Murphey?"

Moments earlier, Palacios had put everyone at home—including Jean—in the three back bedrooms. Now, with a semiautomatic .22-caliber pistol tucked under his belt and Jean's boyfriend standing in front of him, he called over to the others in the car, inviting them in, too. They declined. Palacios and Murphey confronted each other.

"I'm taking Jean with me," Murphey said in a loud voice.

"Over my dead body," Palacios retorted. He pulled out his gun and shot Dennis Murphey four times at point-blank range. Murphey's last words were, "Oh my God, stop!"

But Palacios did not stop. Instead, he went outside and shot at the car. Some of the passengers lay flat, a couple jumped over the sides and scattered, and Gary Inman, who had turned 18 a month earlier, started to drive away. Palacios shot him twice from behind, killing him as the convertible crashed into a nearby parked car. The sergeant went back inside his house and found a dead Dennis Murphey lying face up on the floor. He pumped two more rounds into him. Murphey suffered one shot in the face, two in the neck, and two in what they euphemistically call "the pelvic region." Inman had been hit in the back of the head and the neck. In the fracas, Palacios accidentally shot himself in the left knee. Military Police rushed to the scene; the sheriff's department came out to investigate, cleaned up the mess, and the bodies of Murphey and Inman were hauled away.

At the time, Tucson residents could still easily recall the celebrated case of a few years earlier involving Charles Schmid, a popular, creepy thug appealing to young losers and innocents, who with two of the former had brutally slain three of the latter. When the scope of his activities was revealed, it brought on civic embarrassment and introspection. The Palacios incident, coming just a few years later, provoked even more talk:

"They had it coming."

"Yes, but you can't just go around killing like that."

"I bet his daughter will behave now."

"Pity about the driver."

"But they were smoking marijuana."

"My God, he invited them to his home. It was premeditated."

The press, from the first report, referred to Murphey as a "hippie-type." And the clean-shaven Gary Inman, according to the sheriff's department, drove "a hippie-type vehicle." A clunker? Yes. A poor man's auto? Certainly. But a hippie-type vehicle? No. That would be a Volkswagen van with colorful swirls of peace symbols and flowers painted on the sides and a poorly wrought but recognizable Jimi Hendrix in one corner, Maher Baba in another, and a wavy purple psychedelic "LOVE" scrawled in the middle. Let's get our stereotypes straight here.

Within days, the Pima County Sheriff's Department reported that "a group of hippies are plotting an attempt on Palacios's life and possibly planning to kill a U.S. Air Force military policeman in retaliation." Security was tightened around the base and Palacios himself, then receiving treatment at the base hospital for his self-inflicted wound. Six visitors, "attired in hippie dress and wearing long hair," came to the base hoping to call on the distressed Jean Palacios, but authorities turned them away. More contentious information came from the sheriff's office: Investigators had found "a very long, sharp knife and a long ax handle shaved to a very sharp point" in Inman's car.

It remained for *The Frumious Bandersnatch,* a local biweekly, to portray the range of attitudes in Murphey's community and get first-person accounts. "Sergeant Palacios had reloaded and was just firing at anything that moved," said a university freshman who, with a friend named Gene, had gone along that night for the ride. "I ran with Gene to a house pleading for help. People turned us away from their doors." Another fellow who went on that trip said, "People...don't realize how close they came to having half of this town brought down around their ears." A young woman who lived at the Helen Street house told the *Bandersnatch,* "Palacios better get what he deserved. No matter where the punishment comes from, I want him to get his due. As for Jean, my best friend, my partner...she's a good chick." Said another, "I remember Dennis as a brother who loved all of us, and try and find that forgiveness for his murderer." And finally, this from a housemate: "If Sergeant Palacios gets away with this, we'll bring the whole town down and that's no lie." Murphey's friends were upset that his beard had been shaved and his hair cut for the funeral.

The Helen Street crowd and others who felt outraged at the circumstance were too disorganized and inarticulate to raise any issues about justice and prejudice with the public. Palacios, released on crutches from the hospital after six weeks, was jailed briefly on two counts of murder, then released on his own recognizance. After a week of legal maneuvering, he was back in the county jail awaiting a late September trial.

The prosecution had an open-and-shut case. It had witnesses, motive, and a smoking gun. Palacios had Jack Redhair, a former prosecutor asked by the county to represent the sergeant. He couldn't claim that Palacios had been out of town, or that someone else had pulled the trigger. Redhair's dilemma was simple: How do you justify both shootings? The only defense was insanity. The Air Force psychiatrist thought the insanity dodge might reduce the verdict from first- to second-degree murder, so Redhair looked elsewhere. The prosecutor's best witnesses were dead or longhairs. Palacios's 15-year-old daughter, who had stumbled upon the murder scene while returning to the house with a neighbor, would be a witness, but the county attorney's best testimony would come from Jean and from Palacios himself—if he took the stand.

The Palacios case remained Topic A throughout the summer, but in the uncomfortably hot Sonoran Desert most conversation amounted to little more than shaken heads and clucked tongues. In the Air Force, the case became known far and wide. A fellow I met just the other day who was stationed in Puerto Rico at the time told me he and the others there were practically getting day-by-day reports. *Easy Rider* came out that July, and a major antiwar push by the National Mobilization to End the War in Vietnam kept many occupied; we even convinced a Davis-Monthan airman to speak at a local rally. The Woodstock music festival in mid-August gave alternative lifestyles national exposure. And Sergeant Palacios, fearing a guilty verdict would scotch his accumulated pension, resigned from the Air Force.

Whom did you support? If you drew a line down the middle of a sheet of paper, one side would have these characteristics: military lifer, patriotic, father, religious, traditional, loyal, straight arrow. The other side of the line? Long hair, unkempt, uncommunicative, smoked dope, dropped acid, dropped out, unconventional lifestyle.

Recently Jack Redhair told me this about the jury: "I got an older, bigoted jury and presented the case so Palacios represented everything good about the world and the deceased represented everything bad. The jury knew little about drugs except they were horrible. I showed that the deceased and their friends were panhandlers, not working, pregnant, and that the car had a rope around it to keep the doors shut. And that they wore beads and mustaches. I tried to get the jury to accept that drugs caused this dysfunctional family." Redhair made sure that the published boast from Murphey's friends about bringing the whole town down got before the jury.

Francisco Palacios's 15-year-old daughter, who gave a full statement to investigators the morning after the murders, took the stand and remembered very little about that night. A lieutenant colonel testified in uniform, praising Palacios for his exceptional character and ability. "You could almost hear 'The Star-Spangled Banner' in the courtroom," Redhair recalled more than three decades later. Two civilian psychiatrists who had examined Palacios took the stand to opine that he was not mentally responsible at the time of the killings. And Palacios testified on his own behalf about how frantic he had been that his daughter was living with drug addicts. He started sobbing. He said that Murphey had threatened to kill to get Jean back. He recalled only his first shot—the one that hit his own knee. "After that I can't remember how many shots were fired or who had the gun or anything." Jean took the stand, too, and said that Murphey would pick her up after work and that they'd "just ride around and smoke marijuana." She said she'd taken "about 25 LSD trips" with Murphey.

The trial took place in Pima County's wonderful old two-story courthouse with a Moorish dome atop it, a building that got regular exposure in the mid-1970s during the opening scenes of the weekly television drama "Petrocelli." In his closing argument, Pima County Attorney William Schafer acknowledged that Palacios was a good human being and that Murphey was a tough, bad guy. But that didn't change the facts. Defense attorney Redhair offered the mattress defense: "Think of this father when he went to bring his daughter home, seeing hippies with mattresses on their backs walking in and out of the house."

The jury got the case on Thursday afternoon. After selecting a foreman, they took a straw vote: Nine for not guilty, three not sure. No one voted to convict. Judge Norman Fenton had offered a wide range of options, with guilty of murder at one end, not guilty at the other, and not guilty by reason of temporary insanity in the mix. He instructed his jurors not to be swayed "by sympathy, passion, or prejudice." The jury talked about the insanity option a bit, and one woman stated that she would support "whatever it takes to get Sergeant Palacios home by 6 p.m. to have dinner with his family." In two hours the jury came back with its verdict: not guilty by reason of temporary insanity on both counts. Palacios could go home for dinner with his family. The mattress defense had worked.

Losing prosecutor Schafer called it jury nullification—lawyer jargon for a jury decision based on factors outside the law and the evidence. Winning defendant Palacios said, "This reaffirms my faith in American justice."

Palacios's .22-caliber semiautomatic pistol, a crucial exhibit in the trial, was returned to him a few weeks later. Gary Inman's teenage widow sued the former sergeant for killing her husband. They had been married less than one year and had an infant daughter; now she had no one to support her and the baby. Palacios settled out of court, and over time made regular payments totaling approximately $5,000.

I wrote a short summary of the case for *Hard Times,* a small East Coast weekly. Among its readers was movie director Elia Kazan, who wrote asking if I'd mind sending him my notes and clippings. I didn't send him my notes, but I did send him a few clippings. That a man of his stature and talent had expressed interest in my little piece flattered me—even if I also felt discomfort about Kazan's having named names before the House Committee on Un-American Activities.

A few weeks later, the phone rang.

"Hello, Miller? This is Kazan. I'm at the airport. How do I get out to your place?"

I'm a cheap date; worse, it appears, I'll go out with just about anybody. Kazan came over to my house and we talked about the case, then drove past many of the places in the drama. I still didn't know any of the Helen Street crowd, but I knew a fellow named John who did.

"John what?" Kazan asked. I didn't know John's last name.

"Where does he live?" I didn't know that either. I only knew he spent his afternoons at Himmel Park, by then dubbed Hippie Park. Kazan doubted we could locate someone whose last name and address were unknown. Yet as we pulled up to Himmel Park, there stood John—who, as it happened, did indeed know some of the Helen Street crowd.

Kazan returned to town often, schmoozing with the judge, both attorneys, and Air Force officials. He went to parties, passed joints, and gained the confidence of everyone he met. He ordered a complete set of transcripts from the trial. I asked him once about his shameful appearance before HUAC. "I did what I considered the right thing to do," he said, and offered no regrets.

Kazan did his homework—I did some of his homework, too—and the result was *The Assassins,* a somewhat overwrought but not bad novel based on the Palacios case—and, to a lesser extent, other similar incidents around the country. While Kazan was researching and the rest of us had gone our separate ways, the Peter Boyle movie *Joe* came out. Though not expressly based on the Palacios case, *Joe* had similar elements. It was a busy time for fathers enraged over wayward daughters.

Out at Davis-Monthan Air Force Base, Vandenberg Village has changed its name to the far more resident-friendly Kachina Village. The "PEACE IS OUR PROFESSION" sign has long since been taken down. And on Helen Street, Murphey's old house still stands. From the outside, it looks like a young couple lives there, and the place has been spruced up rather smartly.

~

Cruelty often comes without warning and takes many guises. I've told the story of David Grundman's untimely death to hundreds of people over the years, and not one of them has expressed sorrow. His killer gets all the sympathy. To fully appreciate the showdown that early February afternoon in 1982, let's go back 125 years earlier. James Buchanan succeeds Franklin Pierce as president, Louis Pasteur proves that living organisms cause fermentation, and the U.S. Supreme Court hands down the Dred Scott decision. In the western part of the New Mexico Territory, gold is discovered along the Gila River. Anglo trappers from back East have already made an appearance along some rivers. Mexicans, whose patria had lost two-thirds of its territory to the United States the previous decade, are manipulated out of their land and their labor. And just south of what's now called the Hieroglyphic Mountains, in the northern reaches of the Sonoran Desert, a saguaro cactus seedling, one of some 40 million from the same plant, takes root.

Saguaros have been on earth an estimated 10,000 years, and although they have come to symbolize the rugged and boundless West, they live only within the Sonoran Desert. In the United States this means in Arizona, with precious few interlopers east of the Peloncillo Mountains in New Mexico or across the Colorado River in California. We have a national park out here devoted to the saguaro, and caricatures from Playboy bunnies to Snoopy's brother, Spike, have leaned against them for national exposure.

To say that our seedling that fell in 1857 took root is too hopeful. First, saguaro flowers have to fertilize each other, a process that occurs when a bat or a white-wing dove or other bird carries the nectar from one plant to another. This can happen only during a five-week period in late spring and early summer when the flower opens its white petals at night, exposing its pollen, only to close up the next afternoon in time for *Oprah*. Several weeks later the flower gives way to a lusty, juicy fruit with red pulp that some birds find irresistibly delicious. Its sweet taste has been likened to a cross between a watermelon and a fig. The saguaro fruit that falls to the ground gets eaten by any number of creatures, from insects to small critters on up the chain. No matter who eats the fruit, though, bird or land-walker, its seeds are defecated throughout the desert.

Let's name our seedling Ha:san (pronounced *hah-shīñ*), the word for saguaro within the Tohono O'odham Nation, which exalts the cactus in its traditions, ceremonies, and lore. For Ha:san to actually germinate requires a wide range of natural conditions to fall into place in a given sequence during a finite period of time. These include, over the precious first couple of years, good rainfall, the absence of freezing temperatures, a larger plant nearby to protect the seedling from too much direct sun, and the good fortune to stay out of the way of a jackrabbit or rodent or any animal that, merely by bumping into Ha:san, would kill it. I asked George Montgomery, chief horticulturist at the Arizona-Sonora Desert Museum, how big the saguaro would be if all these conditions held for two years. He took my pen and paper and made a speck no bigger than the period at the end of this sentence.

We're up to 1859 now. *A Tale of Two Cities* comes out, Oregon becomes a state, and John Brown is hanged for leading the raid on the federal arsenal at Harpers Ferry. More germane to our drama, however, Charles Darwin's *On the Origin of Species by Natural Selection* is published. After its second birthday, little Ha:san can relax slightly. True, its life would be over if a cow stepped on it, but now the night temperature can dip below freezing and Ha:san will still be alive the next morning. For a number of years it manages to avoid cow hooves, hungry rabbits, excessive sun, and prolonged frost.

The year Ha:san celebrates its tenth birthday, Walt Whitman publishes *Leaves of Grass*. In Europe, Karl Marx brings out *Das Kapital*. Although the Civil War has come and gone, misguided troops loyal to the Confederacy skirmish with a U.S. Cavalry scouting party at Picacho Pass, 80 miles south of Ha:san's desert land. Of zero significance to Ha:san, the U.S. Congress has now divided the New Mexico Territory in two; Ha:san's half is called Arizona. At age ten, Ha:san stands one-and-a-half inches tall. Four years later the first known photograph of a saguaro is taken, not too far west of Ha:san's dwelling place.

By age 30, in 1887, Ha:san has grown to a sturdy two feet tall. Prescott is the territory's capital, an honor soon shifted to Phoenix. Arizona's five-year Pleasant Valley War begins, a violent conflict over sheep and cattle and turf and family dominance. Ha:san has no enemies; though still a young cactus, it has survived its most vulnerable years. In March of Ha:san's 44th year, Ha:san and its species get friendly news: The saguaro blossom is named Arizona's territorial flower. Finally, at age 55 in 1912, the year that Arizona gains statehood, Ha:san claims another level of maturity for itself: A crown of Arizona's flower grows on its top for the first time, providing nectar for its airborne visitors. Soon seedlings from Ha:san's own fruit will reach the desert floor. Ha:san stands eight feet tall now, closer to the popular image of a saguaro. None of its 39,999,999 sibling seedlings made it this far.

Ha:san has an easy life. Statehood schmatehood, no one bothers the growing saguaro cactus and it bothers no one. A narrow east-west road a few miles south connects Wickenberg to the west to some small towns much farther east, but Ha:san remains secure in the desert with bald eagles and great blue herons flying about and rattlers and Western diamondbacks slithering below. Other cactus such as ocotillo and prickly pear and trees such as ironwood and paloverde live nearby. Mule deer and wild burros trot by on occasion, and coyotes and rabbits are regular passersby. Ha:san weighs 800 pounds by now, 90 percent of which is water sucked up from the ground. It is landlord to the Gila woodpecker, which bores out a hole in its skin big enough for a nest; when the woodpecker moves on, elf owls, curve-billed thrashers, and cactus wrens move in.

Saguaro cactus

Ha:san's biggest breakthrough takes place about the same time. It starts to grow arms. The arms take on some of the same characteristics as the trunk—slow growing, with flowers eventually blossoming at the ends and with woodpeckers and other birds as permanent guests.

In 1933 at age 76, Ha:san is at the peak of its form. Mature, one arm growing nicely and another on the way, plenty of water to drink in the rainy season and retain through the dry season, its outer pleats evenly spaced, birds at home among its needles. It is the first year of the New Deal and the last year the Washington Senators win the American League pennant. Almost a quarter of a century later—in Ha:san's centennial year—Jack Kerouac's *On the Road* is published, the Brooklyn Dodgers move to Los Angeles, and David Michael Grundman is born in New York State.

We know far more about Ha:san's formative years than we do about Grundman's. Let's give him the benefit of a doubt and assume he graduated from high school. At age 21 Grundman lived in Johnson City, a New York town near the Pennsylvania border three-and-a-half hours northwest of Manhattan. In the middle of the winter he lured a 16-year-old boy to a friend's apartment, intent on stealing the lad's $1,200—money with which the kid hoped to buy three pounds of marijuana. Grundman pulled a gun on the boy but botched the job, and he was arrested for armed robbery. A day before he was to go on trial, he agreed to a plea bargain: He would plead guilty to second-degree robbery, which carried a maximum sentence of four years, rather than stand trial and risk a more severe sentence. On January 29, 1981, after 18 months in Attica, David Michael Grundman was released on parole.

He stood six-one, with brown hair and blue eyes, and weighed 200 pounds. By the end of the year, he and a buddy named Jim Suchocki—who had been arrested for possessing a nice quantity of marijuana a few years earlier—had moved to the Southwest. Grundman's mother lived in a quiet working-class neighborhood in northwest Phoenix, and the two moved in with her. They were 53 miles southwest of Ha:san.

About this time I lived in a small adobe adjoining the Tucson Botanical Gardens. It was a tranquil and captivating place, surrounded by thick desert growth that absorbed noisy traffic and blocked nosy neighbors. Late one midsummer afternoon I discovered a Papago woman a few yards from my house brandishing a long saguaro rib. (This was before the tribe changed its name from Papago to Tohono O'odham.) I recall her name as Henrietta. Saguaro ribs—sturdy, lightweight, woody poles that grow within the cactus's trunk—are used to lift, or sometimes knock, the fruit off the top of tall saguaros. The ribs, which litter the desert floor as part of decaying saguaro carcasses, are also used in home and fence construction. To simplify gathering the fruit, the far end of one rib is often fashioned into a two-pronged fork; to extend their length, two ribs are frequently strapped together. I stood and watched admiringly as the woman delicately lifted one fruit after another off the tops of saguaros and handed them to her young daughter, who carefully placed each in a plastic bucket. Finally Henrietta noticed me and smiled as I complimented her on her ability to lift the fruit from the plant.

Proprietorship was no concern; I was a mere Anglo renter, and this harvesting of the saguaro fruit was an ancient tradition in her tribe. The saguaro even played a role in their creation stories. A teacher I know grew up on the Tohono O'odham reservation with Papago as his first language. "I used to take my bow and arrow as a kid," he told me, "and shoot at the saguaro. My grandfather said, 'Don't do that. All things are alive. That plant is very special to the O'odham. It bears fruit that we use for food. When Mother Earth decides not to give any more life to the saguaro, we use its ribs for many things.'"

In a manner both gallant and sociable, Henrietta asked if I would like a jar of saguaro jelly once she boiled the pulp down into syrup. (Most syrup is fermented for wine, to be used in ceremonial gatherings on the reservation.) That was our bond; we parted all smiles. For weeks I told anyone who would listen this little episode about the friendly encounter with the saguaro-gatherer in my yard. When Henrietta had not returned by late fall, however, I realized I would never taste saguaro jelly from the cactus beside my house.

On February 4, 1982, David Grundman didn't go to work at the Sun Kountry Kitchen. Instead, he and Jim Suchocki headed out into the desert an hour northeast of Phoenix with lots of beer, a 16-gauge shotgun, a box of rifle slugs, and their dog. It was a weekday with temperatures in the comfortable mid-60s. They drove toward Wickenberg through swap-meet country, over the railroad tracks leading to Los Angeles, and past Del Webb's Sun City. The only town they passed was Surprise. At Route 74, the Carefree Road, they turned east 12.7 miles and then north on a dirt road into Bureau of Land Management desert land. After bouncing along the road a couple of miles, they parked the car and walked east a bit, settling in near an arroyo full of wolfberry shrubs and squat mesquite trees. Instead of the usual incessant weekend noise of all-terrain vehicles tearing up the land, all the two could hear was desert. They had the Sonoran Desert to themselves, or at least that swatch of it. On north-facing slopes grew jojoba; on south, saguaro. Some were younger, shorter, and lighter than Ha:san; others were older, taller, and heavier.

After a few beers, David Grundman started shooting. At saguaros. They made easy, immobile targets, almost humanlike with their arms in the air. He began with smaller saguaros and worked up to bigger ones, each time shooting the cactus enough so that the *Carnegiea gigantea* fell over dead.

"The first one was easy," he told Jim after killing two saguaros, "and the larger one was partly dead already." In the silent desert, the final fall of each cactus must have resounded thunderous. Javelina, common there at that time of the year, stayed away from the drunken marksman. Grundman must have killed a half-dozen saguaros, leaving each one lying on the ground as he moved to the next.

Finally David Grundman encountered Ha:san. A couple of rounds didn't do it. Ha:san, 125 years old, remained erect. Grundman moved slightly to another angle and pumped a few more slugs into the splendid 3,000-pound saguaro, but it refused to fall. He tried again from farther over. In all, he moved about a third of the way around Ha:san. Frustrated at this particular cactus's resistance to his gunshots and determined to best it, Grundman picked up a saguaro rib from the ground and started poking at Ha:san's lowest arm, which had grown almost five feet in its 70 years. Grundman's poking finally dislodged the arm, which rested about four feet above him and weighed close to 500 pounds.

Well, the joke was on David Grundman, and so was Ha:san. The arm crashed down on him, and the 25-foot trunk of the mighty cactus, suddenly unstable, started wobbling. It could have fallen anywhere in a 360-degree radius, but it too fell square on David Grundman. His last word was, "Jim!"

I've never given much thought to retribution or karma, yet surely both of those were at work in the Sonoran Desert on February 4, 1982. David Michael Grundman lay face-up, dead beneath a ton and a half and 125 years of cactus, saguaro needles piercing his face and torso. Natural selection had played its hand.

Jim Suchocki, full of beer and bravado, went into momentary shock, then ran over and rolled the cactus off his dead buddy just as a car passed by on the lonely road nearby. Suchocki flagged it down and asked the driver to get someone quick from Lake Pleasant, the Maricopa County park slightly to the east. Grundman was an accidental-gunshot victim, he said. By the time park manager Doug Collup arrived, Jim had gathered up all the beer bottles and rifle slugs and put them in the car with the dog. Collup had called for a helicopter, but when he saw Grundman, he changed that to a hearse. Ha:san's arm had hit David between the neck and shoulder, and the trunk had landed directly on top of him. The side of his face was mashed in and yellow. You could still smell beer around his mouth.

"The cactus probably broke his neck on impact," Collup said when we spoke at his home years after the fact. Collup had returned to the site to photograph it the day after the accident, and he found Grundman's teeth prints still visible in the big cactus.

"See that?" Collup held up one of his photos. "The cactus is reddish from the blood. Some of the needles are bruised and some are missing. The cactus popped his gums like they were little water balloons." The county medical examiner's description for Grundman's cause of death: "external compression of chest."

The falling-cactus story makes for great telling and retelling. Within a few years it had graduated to urban-myth status; people weren't sure if it was true or not, but it had all the elements of a noir morality tale. It has surfaced a few times in print, but only Michael Stevens of the Austin Lounge Lizards and a friend have artfully immortalized Ha:san and his calamitous end by composing a ballad. "Saguaro" appears on the Lounge Lizards' album *Creatures from the Black Saloon.* It turns the affair into a Western in which Grundman *("a noxious little twerp")* sees himself as Wyatt Earp to the saguaro's Clanton gang. At the end, though, the roles are reversed: *"One mighty arm of justice came hurtling toward the ground."*

Guided by the initial sheriff's reports and Collup's memory, I set out one day to locate the scene of the crime. I started at the house where Grundman had lived in northwest Phoenix, trying to emulate his last journey, but nothing along the way encouraged a warped and wasted mind. A billboard said, "KEEP DRIVING IF YOU LOVE AVOCADOS." As I neared my goal, I ran into construction for a new golf course and had to park the car and go on foot. After hiking north up and down small hills for a mile or two, I found a bone-dry arroyo with a lightly sloping, south-facing stretch on the other side. It was the sort of desolate spot where *Bloodbath at Massacre Creek* might have been filmed had anyone ever filmed a movie called *Bloodbath at Massacre Creek.* During late-summer monsoons, arroyos like this one can fill up quicker than your Maytag. Some Bud Light cans lay nearby; tangled in the scrub was the bullet-riddled side of a Remington game load box.

Dead saguaros disintegrate within a few years, and I wasn't exactly expecting to find Ha:san's corpse or even its ribs. But I did look at the surrounding saguaros in a new light. There was no logic behind it, but I stepped lightly when I got near them, and I never ventured close enough that one of them could fall on me if it wanted to. They were part of Ha:san's extended family, and I simply wanted to pay my respects.

CHAPTER 7

THE FREE STATE OF COCHISE

~

I. BORDER DISORDER

One Tuesday morning I found myself among the painfully righteous. There was Joan, Jack, Emilie, and Alva, who showed up late, and Mary, who arrived just before we finished. We were picking up trash in the desert scrub near High Lonesome Road where it cuts off of Double Adobe Road at Arizona Highway 80. A couple of Tuesdays previous, more than a dozen trash-picker-uppers had answered the call, and once a visiting high-school group from Kentucky had swelled the crowd. But this Tuesday's crew was dishearteningly small.

We started out at 7 a.m., before the sun's rays forced us back inside. Under slightly different circumstances, we might have been one of the ubiquitous Adopt-a-Highway cleanup crews, toiling on behalf of a Rotary Club or Charlene's Hair 'n' Nails. But the stretch we had adopted was one that Mexicans and others from south of the border traveled in their first few hours in the United States, if they entered without papers. The expanse was part of a labyrinth of trails, paths, arroyos, and rangeland every bit as complex as the nationwide interstate highway system. In fact, you could make a case for calling it the international highway system: It starts in

Central America, and more and more travelers come on board as it moves north through Mexico. By the time it reaches 31° 20" North latitude—the U.S.-Mexico border from New Mexico's boot heel west to Nogales, where the east-west border crooks slightly north—many thousands have joined the journey.

The northbound procession pauses in Agua Prieta, Sonora, where guides called *polleros* routinely sign up participants, known as *pollos* or chickens, for every peso they carry, then send them across the frontier on the outskirts of Agua Prieta, which abuts Douglas, Arizona. It is the task of the U.S. Border Patrol, based in Douglas, to capture these border crossers and send them back across the line. To the Border Patrol, they are UDAs and OTMs, Undocumented Aliens and Other Than Mexicans. (No one uses "wetback" anymore in public.) The crossers who elude the Border Patrol, estimated at more than 80 percent, head to safe houses and pickup points, where they crowd into cars, vans, or trucks waiting to take them as far and as fast from the border as possible.

Between the border and the pickup point miles away, these hundreds upon hundreds a night finish off plastic water bottles, throw away odds and ends filling their pockets, shed clothes, and cook food over makeshift campfires. The stream of trash they leave behind looks unsightly and adds to the irritation that ranchers, whose land they cross, already feel. So I joined Joan, Jack, Emilie, and Alva, who showed up late, and Mary, who arrived just before we finished, in dutifully picking up trash newly discarded in the United States. If Mother Teresa had lived in Cochise County, Arizona, she would have come on Tuesday mornings, too.

Osmopura. Judging from the number of plastic water jugs we picked up, the Osmopura company is profiting nicely from the southern influx. And in Agua Prieta, whose economy has rapidly adjusted to the crush of travelers arriving daily by second-class bus, Osmopura is doing very well in both the half-liter, three-peso (28¢) size and the full-liter, four-peso (37¢) size. "A Proudly Mexican Product," boasts the label. Sometimes polleros will supply sandwiches to their apprehensive pollos before they set out, though they have found that geography interferes with diet: Pollos from southern Mexico don't eat Pan Bimbo, a Wonder Bread–like white bread, so the polleros prepare tortas for them using smaller, puffier bread with a thicker crust.

The section of Agua Prieta closest to the United States has undergone a major transformation. Where once you found shops for tourists, small restaurants, and local businesses, now the streets are cheek by jowl with flophouses squeezing as many $4-a-night northbound transients into a room as possible. Librolandia—a bookstore I was fond of—and a favorite boot shop across the street are among the many stores that have been sacrificed on the altar of northbound travel.

Border towns once had *escritores publicos* who, for a modest fee, would help non-literates compose, then type out, letters to their homes in the interior. Now Western Union is filled all day with northbound migrants sending that last message home and picking up money, and southbound travelers sending money home after a successful season in the field, on a construction site, or in a kitchen. The push and pull of global migration, the startling numbers and personal traumas—all this has changed the very culture of border towns throughout the world, including this unspectacular one that rests on the south side of 31° 20" North latitude.

Not that Agua Prieta has been an innocent port of entry in the past. For many years, the commerce that fueled the city's economy was in smuggling drugs, not humans. Young men with no visible means of support wearing snakeskin boots were highly visible in their shiny new $35,000 off-road 5.9-liter four-wheel-drive V-8 pickups with leather interiors and lower front driving lights. Restaurants and nightclubs opened with proceeds nefariously gained. In all, Agua Prieta has profited handsomely from the marijuana and cocaine trade. Northbound migration is determined by

Immigration inspectors during temporary border closing, Naco, Arizona

where and how extensively the U.S. Border Patrol deploys its troops. If the cities are choked off, then migrants go to the more dangerous and less patrolled desert land.

Drugs coming north simply cross where they can. For a while—until May 1990—they came from Agua Prieta not just overland but under land as well. A well-engineered tunnel, built with good material and malice aforethought, linked Agua Prieta, Mexico, with Douglas, United States. Its Mexican terminus was the poolroom in a private residence. The tunnel, big enough for a human to negotiate, descended 30 feet, proceeded northward for 300 feet, then surfaced in a construction warehouse in Douglas. It had been in use for many months, and its discovery set off violent turf wars within Mexican drug cartels—and quieter ones inside embarrassed American law-enforcement agencies.

Trans-border tunnels are nothing new. When I first traveled the Mexican frontier in the late 1970s, old-time border rats recounted tales of Prohibition-era tunnels established by Chicago gangsters. But the Agua Prieta–Douglas tunnel became the first modern-day underground drug railroad on the border's dry western third. Its revelation inspired those all-American phenomena, T-shirts and bumper stickers. My T-shirt cost ten dollars, and it has a nicely rendered cutaway drawing of the entire subterranean structure, complete with endpoints. The bumper sticker says HANDS UNDER THE BORDER, a spoof on binational friendship events. The residence at the tunnel's southern terminus has since been converted into a skill-training center. The warehouse covering the tunnel's northern terminus is now used by the City of Douglas motor pool; adjacent space has been turned over to a shelter for battered women and children. The tunnel, I've been assured, has been cemented shut on both sides.

The Agua Prieta-Douglas narco-tunnel inspired other similar efforts. So many binational storm drains converted into tunnels have been discovered linking Nogales, Sonora, with Nogales, Arizona, that one recent find inspired the *Nogales International* to proclaim, "ANOTHER DRUG TUNNEL (stock headline number 72)." In 1993, a quarter-mile tunnel crossing into California east of Tijuana was discovered before it could be used. This tunnel, at a depth of 65 feet, came with air conditioning and lighting. The disclosure was "one more blow on the war on drugs," a ranking Border Patrol official proudly said at the time. Just how many such blows would be struck became apparent five years later when, to its chagrin, the Border Patrol discovered that the very same tunnel was being used to smuggle UDAs and OTMs into the United States.

In separate experiments, scientists with the U.S. Army Corps of Engineers and the University of Denver Research Institute have tried to detect tunnels from above ground by electronically searching for irregularities in underground soil and rock density. Thus far, a veteran U.S. Customs official told me, federal agents have found the techniques less than worthwhile.

Picking up trash back on High Lonesome Road, we split up pretty much at random. Each of us carried a large burlap bag donated by the Bisbee Coffee Company. Burlap bags are better to drag through the desert than large Jonathan Winter plastic trash bags because they don't tear when they brush against sharp branches, thorns, and cactuses. The first time the Border Justice Cleanup Crew went out, Safeway supplied bread and sandwich meat, and Ace Hardware gave work gloves. Bisbee Lumber

("YOUR'S...SINCE 1903") donated the plastic bags for sorting the trash at the end.

Joan, a feisty high-school librarian with fire-engine-red toenail polish, headed off to the south side of High Lonesome. Why had she woken up early on a vacation morning to brave the prickly, sweaty, cheerless desert? "I'm here to make a personal statement and do what I can to reduce the tension even a teeny bit," she said.

Emilie, an activist community-college English teacher with deep purple toenails, wandered out on the north side of the road. "I'm trying to do some good in the face of all this ranting," she explained.

Alva, who showed up late and whose toes were covered the entire time, said she was "determined to do something for humanity."

A Border Patrol truck rolled down High Lonesome and we waved at its driver. I started to find Osmopura jugs, rusted silverware, shards of glass, scraps of paper, cans, beer bottles evidently left by youthful American partiers, and—between two limp bushes—a thick foam double mattress in relatively good condition. Emilie saved clothes she picked up, washed them, and took them over to Mexico to distribute to the poor. Her best discovery of the day was a New York Yankees cap; she decided to add it to a planned altar that she and Jack and some others will build from found personal effects such as Bibles, personal identifications, family photos, a phone card, and a child's glove. The effort to clean up the immigrants' garbage got an official send-off at its inception when the Cochise County government lent a hand in coordinating groups throughout the area. In all, crews collected ten tons of debris and recyclables that first weekend.

Our spot next to High Lonesome Road testified to northbound traffic patterns. To get there safely, migrants have to cross into the United States at dusk a few miles outside Agua Prieta, far beyond the western extremity of the U.S.-built border fence, and zigzag northwesterly, keeping Highway 80 in sight. After a while they will see a red neon arrow above Mike's Corral, a steak house not far away on Double Adobe Road. Mike's features decent food, life-size cutouts of John Wayne, and a video game with programmable messages flashing across the screen ("YOUR BARTENDER'S WANDA & SUE"). Its considerable outside lights are a well-known beacon for brand-new immigrants trying to get their bearings; over the years, the parking lot of Mike's has become a rendezvous for smuggler and smuggled alike.

A friend who lives on 55 acres nearby said that until 1997 or '98 he would see one or two Mexicans a year cross his land and head up the arroyo toward the well-lighted Mike's. Now it's not uncommon for 50 or more to pass through every night. "I was so sympathetic and good to them at first," the property owner said. "I'd give them water and food and send them on their way. But now they're back in droves." We hopped in my friend's Jeep and drove to an arroyo on his property where six heavily trafficked trails converged.

"Look at all those footprints. It looks like a convention took place here. A Border Patrol helicopter goes overhead three times a day now. And I heard those cleanup people"—he was speaking of Joan, Jack, Emilie, and Alva, who showed up late, and Mary, who arrived just before we finished—"want to put in port-a-potties and water stations. Why don't they hand out maps while they're at it?"

(In the summer of 2000, with the cooperation of the U.S. Border Patrol, a volunteer group in California placed dozens of full one-gallon water jugs in the desert between San Diego and Calexico, where dehydration has claimed the lives of many migrants. The jugs are marked by 30-foot-high blue flags.)

A little farther on, my friend in the Jeep showed me the hull of his gutted 1969 Cadillac Coupe de Ville convertible that he had kept out in the desert as a parts car for his other Coupe de Ville. "The wets dragged the backseats out of the car, took off the hubcaps and mounted the seats on them, then used them for mattresses. When one of the seats caught fire from their campfire, they ran off and left my car to burn up. It's toast." True, his old Caddy—a car he had owned for close to 15 years—was now a crisp shell with nothing salvageable. "We've trained our dogs to bark now whenever Mexicans come through."

The Caddy owner was calm compared with the rage some felt. For that you could crank up your computer to one of the rancher websites or just drive toward New Mexico on Highway 80 east of Douglas. There you'll see a sign planted on a rancher's spread saying "Tons of Dope, Thousands of Mexicans Pass by This Sign." A little farther on, another one: "Free Trade Policy: Drugs Come North, Money Goes South." A Colorado man was so irate at the situation that he drove to Douglas and, acting as a one-man construction crew, used chain link and concertina wire to extend the border fence westward 40 feet. "It runs through what seems like the only swamp in the state," said an amused friend who saw it. The Border Patrol said they'd have to take down the new addition.

Ranchers have parlayed their helplessness into aggressive vigilantism. A few go out armed, round up Mexicans crossing their land, and turn them over to the Border Patrol. The legal issues get sticky here, touching on property rights, trespass laws, and what you can do with your weapon and what you can't. Ranchers and their supporters have held meetings whose themes were dangerously close to "stomp the Mes'kins." A goon squad from Texas volunteered to come over and help protect America, or at least this stretch of it, from foreigners.

Dunderheads like these Texans crop up every now and then to exploit an already delicate situation. In the mid-1980s, some fools called Civilian Matériel Assistance held "maneuvers" near the Arizona–Sonora border to stop the drug traffic that surely funds global communism. In the late 70s, David Duke and the Klan rumbled through to ignite yet another border conflagration.

There, sitting in the desert about a quarter mile north of High Lonesome Road, I found a gleaming white porcelain toilet bowl. Certainly it was not carried in by immigrants, surely by local teens as a joke. Recalling something vaguely similar at that same age in my own past, I had to laugh. Emilie located a vast hole in the ground in which four abandoned rusting cars were neatly parked side by side. Each one of us, in fact, found something beyond our mission, and that made the saintliness of our task a bit more tolerable.

The town north of the border that has simultaneously benefited and suffered from the black market in its midst is Douglas—for many years a model Phelps Dodge copper town. The P-D Mercantile clothed and fed most townspeople, the smelter employed them, and corporate benevolence soothed them. Although Douglas has had a Mexican-American majority, until recent decades it remained an Anglo-ruled town with implicit segregation. P-D phased out in the 1980s, the victim of enlightened environmental regulations, fluctuating world copper prices, and antiquated equipment.

At the core of the town's power structure sat the Borane brothers, Joe and Ray. The latter was with the local school district, then mayor; the former was police chief, then justice of the peace and city magistrate. In a town of 15,000, these last two positions made him the locus of power—which, coupled with his extensive real estate holdings, anointed Joe Borane a man to be reckoned with.

For years—decades, really—people gossiped about corruption and drug profiteering on Borane's part, but the accusations stayed underground—except for those made on a curious self-produced 45-rpm record sung by the late Miguel "Tamal" Moreno, a Douglas fellow given to arson, drug dealing, and jailhouse law. Tamal's predilection for the first two callings allowed him ample opportunity to practice the third. I was introduced to him at a Douglas bar during one of his occasional interludes out of prison. Tamal was a genuine character, perhaps too clever by half. Once he was satisfied I wasn't a narcotics agent, he opened up with chapter and verse on each of the town fathers and their sins. I wanted a copy of "Joe Cocaine," his 45 about Joe Borane, but he kept putting me off. Later that day, as I sat in the living room of a friend I had impulsively dropped in on, a stranger walked in, handed me a copy of the record, turned around, and left. It's a nice little song with Tamal singing, backed up by only guitar and drums.

Joe Cocaine was the chief of police. He lived in a little town.
He sold his dope and he ran his whores and he paid the sheriff off.
Joe Cocaine, the citizens of our town, they don't want you around.
Joe Cocaine, you better leave town.

The record was played on an Agua Prieta station a few times, but in the States its renown was strictly word of mouth. When Joe Borane was arrested in September 1999 for money laundering and racketeering, investigators found a copy of the record in his office desk.

Lee D. Morgan II winced when I mentioned Tamal, and he winced again when I asked him about Joe Borane. Morgan II is not given to wincing. Quite the opposite; he usually maintains a cool, unflappable posture. When the Texan started out in law enforcement as a border patrolman in the 1970s, he had already taken sniper training in the 101st Airborne. Now, as special agent in charge of the U.S. Customs office in Douglas, his reputation as a cowboy stayed with him. His office is lined with photographs of John Wayne ("They don't make 'em like him anymore"), and a well-known quote from Hemingway ("There is no hunting like the hunting of man") hangs nearby. He travels with an M-16 by his side ("Don't leave home without one"). He is the only law-enforcement man I've ever met who has a Roman numeral after his name. He smokes Marlboro Lights.

On this particular morning, Morgan II had gotten word from a snitch—a "confidential informant"—that a certain fellow in a specific car was going out on Highway 80 east of town to pick up either pollos or dope—he wasn't sure which. The feds surrounded the suspect without his even knowing it. Two Customs vehicles took the lead, leaving Morgan II in his government '98 Ford pickup to bring up the rear. Every few miles he'd stop, pull out his 8x56 binoculars, and spy the suspect half a mile or so in front. The suspect slowed down only once, as he passed mile marker 386 and looked south into the desert. Then he resumed his speed. About 15 miles from the New Mexico line, the advance Customs agents pulled him over to check his license and registration. He was clean, so they sent him on his way.

The car's paper trail, by contrast, was classic smuggler. It had been sold at an auction in Arizona the previous week, taken into Mexico where clean ownership documents were generated, and sent back into the States for a pickup. The Customs guys searched the desert near mile marker 386 but came back empty-handed. The next day, however, they returned to 386; this time they found 250 pounds of marijuana in the desert.

In fiscal 1998, Morgan II's office seized more than 27,000 pounds of marijuana, a figure that jumped to 40,000 pounds the following year. He volunteered only one observation all morning. "The drought's been real nasty lately," he offered as we passed Silver Creek east of Douglas, "but I see the cottonwood trees are still green near the bottom."

Mary, who arrived just before we finished picking up migrant garbage, helped us sort the recyclables from the just plain trash. It was 9:45, the heat was too much, and the no-see-ums too many. We drove over to Dot's Diner for breakfast.

II. DEPORTABLE

I went to jail on my first visit to Bisbee. A friend had been impris-
oned there for antiwar activity, and to cheer him up a bunch of us
hopped in a van and drove 95 miles southeast from Tucson to the
Cochise County lockup. Ernie was released after a few weeks, but
the town captivated me.

The jail was housed on the top floor of the county courthouse,
a terrific WPA-era art deco building in a section of town originally
settled by businessmen and their families during the first wave of
copper mining toward the end of the 19th century and the
beginning of the 20th. The neighborhood was called Quality Hill
for its pristine air, and some of its early houses still stand, painstak-
ingly restored and nicely maintained. Just up the street from the
courthouse stands the Bisbee Woman's Club, spelled that way
because, I've always assumed, Bisbee women are indeed singular.

The Phelps Dodge Company was still extracting ore from the
ground in 1971 when Ernie was in temporary residence, then
shipping it 20 miles to Douglas for smelting. Bisbee was still a
womb-to-tomb company town: Cradles were bought at the Phelps
Dodge Mercantile, and doctors pronounced you dead at the company hospital. And the union was still viable. The shift-change
whistle pierced the air three times a day, a reminder of who ran the
town and how. And although P-D had announced it was phasing
out operations in four or five years, few merchants or miners
planned ahead with that prospect in mind. The twin qualities of
Phelps Dodge—paternalism in civic matters and intransigence in
labor relations—were known and accepted. In a region of the

country known for cycles of boom and bust, Bisbee had boomed
for so long it scarcely knew from bust.

P-D's coitus interruptus after generations of fatherly sway left
the town in a stupor. Bisbee did not become a ghost town
overnight, but it did take on skeletal qualities. The county government became the leading employer. Merchants sold their stock
and boarded up their stores on their way out of town; miners
who couldn't sell their homes left them in the hands of others to
take the first offer that came along. A lot of the homes were in sad
condition, and many old canyonside shacks needed new foundations, plumbing, wiring, insulation, roofs, windows, walls, ceilings,
and floors. Some dilapidated two-bedroom hovels were selling for
$500 each.

Phelps Dodge left a few workers to oversee its extensive holdings and continue leaching operations, in which the substantial
tailings piled up on the edge of town were wrung once again
for that last ounce of low-grade ore. The businessmen who
remained—a landfill operator, grocers, insurance agents—continued to operate as if P-D was still in charge, though in fact nobody
was. It was this power vacuum that appealed mightily to the next
generation of Bisbeeites—not to fill it, but to preserve it as best
they could.

The new pioneers straggled into the Cochise County seat by
ones and twos, arriving in VW vans and secondhand pickups from
throughout the West—and, as word dribbled out, the country at
large. They were determinedly bad artists, newly divorced women in
their first retail enterprise, self-absorbed poets, semiretired bikers,

tuneless musicians and toolless carpenters, alcoholic Vietnam vets, mild-mannered dopers, shifty ne'er-do-wells with new sets of IDs, panhandlers with no one to panhandle, the overeducated and the underfinanced, unreconstructed hippies and reconstituted New Ageists, Earth mothers and wayward fathers, underage runaways and trust-fund babies, burned-out politicos and would-be commies. They suffered from acute NVMS (No Visible Means of Support), and they meant to keep it that way, by God.

Word had gotten out that there was no work in Bisbee, and that attracted more people. The town became a rest stop on the gringo trail that wound through North America, down into Mexico, and on into Central America all the way south to Tierra del Fuego. This was no Sedona, with its crystal alchemy and power vortices, nor was it the California dream of the Mamas and the Papas. What they saw was what they got.

What they got as they approached on Highway 80 was a beat-up old mining town in well-defined sections spread all over the landscape. The core, Old Bisbee, never failed to startle first-time visitors with its narrow, twisting streets, its tin-roofed houses precariously positioned on angular hillsides, its steep cement stairs that no mail carrier dared to climb. The gentle breeze blowing through town seemed to come from the WPA era. If you arrived from the west, you passed through a tunnel at the top of Mule Mountain and gasped at the difference between what you had left behind and what you saw before you; coming from the east, you would have driven around the monstrous mined-out Lavender Pit and come to what initially appeared to be a European gingerbread village.

Although it sits less than ten miles from Mexico, Bisbee wore a miner's hard hat rather than a border-town sombrero. Even so, many considered Cochise County closer to Mexico than the United States, though it pretty much ignored the laws of both. Bisbee was the capital of what some called the Free State of Cochise—a mix of ornery cultures linked by geography and independence. All of this has made for an entirely comfortable place to write, and that's what I've done there, intermittently, as the town has shifted personalities while retaining its essential integrity.

Although the mid-1970s onslaught of hippies, transients, and counterculture migrants brought inevitable complications, the residue of Bisbee's power structure did its best to shoo them out of town as quickly as they arrived. This suspicion of outsiders was nothing new: For more than half a century after Bisbee's original settlement around 1880, Chinese learned in no uncertain terms that they had best move on past sundown.

The town's biggest and most ghastly eviction, however, took place in 1917 during the War to End All Wars in the middle of Woodrow Wilson's administration, when agitators from the Industrial Workers of the World (IWW) accused the mining companies of war profiteering and organized a major strike. Cochise County Sheriff Harry Wheeler, acting on behalf of mining interests that saw the IWW as backers of Germany, deputized a Loyalty League and sent it out at daybreak to round up strikers, sympathizers, and anyone deemed to be a supporter.

By midday that hot July 12, some 2,000 miners had been marched the four miles from Bisbee to the Warren Mining District baseball park. Given one last chance to repent—that is, to renounce the strike—more than half refused to back down. Their reward was a sweltering boxcar ride east on the Phelps Dodge-owned El Paso and Southwestern into the godforsaken Chihuahuan Desert. There they were let out near remote Hermanas, New Mexico, a watering station on the railroad line and not much more.

Most of the deportees never made it back to Bisbee; the few who did had to sneak into town and change their names. Management's abhorrent approach to strike-busting worked. Later a presidential inquiry headed by not-yet Supreme Court Justice Felix Frankfurter simply shook a disapproving finger at the sheriff. Of course the damage had been done, and both camps—miners and management—acquired reputations that linger to this day. Bisbee, for its part, gained notoriety as a town where you don't trifle with corporate authority.

The Bisbee Deportation never gets its due in American history textbooks, but for a number of years in the 1980s and into the 90s, the personal became political and historical as well. A friendly, genuine card-carrying IWW member, Rob e. Hanson, had moved to town. Hanson, an angular fellow then in his 60s, opened up a Wobbly printshop in Bisbee's Lowell District, a strip of largely abandoned storefronts on the rim of the Lavender Pit. Lowell had once been residential, but the town contracted as the pit expanded, leaving only a hardware store, a laundromat, a bar, a pool hall, and an artist's studio. Rob e. Hanson's research rediscovered Jim Brew, an unemployed miner who had moved from Colorado to a rooming house in Bisbee in World War I. On the day of the deportation, instead of allowing himself to be rounded up or even questioned, Brew shot and killed an approaching deputized thug named Orson McRae—who, according to Phelps Dodge literature, had been unarmed. Brew himself was immediately killed by McRae's cohorts. Brew was the only miner who died in the entire deportation drama; McRae's was the only death on management's side.

I came to know Rob e. Hanson in his dual roles of anarcho-syndicalist and printer. In a fit of solidarity with the Industrial Workers of the World, and wanting the infamous IWW bug on something, I ordered some stationery from his Signature Press. Solidarity schmolidarity—the bug was there all right, but the printing was slightly off-center and the inking was uneven. I never asked Rob e. Hanson why he lowercased his middle initial; I suppose he figured a man just shouldn't accumulate too much capital.

Hanson held graveside services every year for Jim Brew, a noble effort to draw attention to the whole deportation affair. He gave deputy McRae his due, too: "Both men were the victims of a corporate policy bent on destroying the union movement in America." A few dozen of us would show up at Evergreen Cemetery each year, where Hanson would lay a wreath on Brew's headstone. Occasionally there were remarks by guest speakers—either Wobblies from out of town or local attorney Jon Pintek, whose father (a miner-turned-taxi driver) had been taken at gunpoint from his home on deportation day but eventually let go. One year the Arizona Rangers held a service honoring Sheriff Harry Wheeler in the same cemetery. Speaking of Wheeler, Hanson said: "I love him as much as I do James Brew. It's the event I deplore."

No monument or roadside historical plaque commemorates the Bisbee Deportation. Except for the novel *Bisbee '17* by Robert Houston, it has never achieved the national notoriety of other episodes on the Southwest labor-history circuit. DVDs and CD-ROMs and at least three books enlighten the public about the *Salt of the Earth* labor struggle in Silver City, New Mexico.

But then there's the famous 1914 Ludlow Massacre.

In 1914 in Ludlow, Colorado, striking United Mine Workers and their families were slaughtered by the National Guard. The event has become known for its sheer horror and its personification by the Rockefellers, who owned the struck coal mine and engineered the bloodbath. Woody Guthrie wrote a song, "Ludlow Massacre," about the atrocity. The United Mine Workers maintains a monument near Interstate 25 in southern Colorado between Aguilar and Trinidad on the spot where the National Guard attacked the strikers' tent encampment after a growing and protracted strike. It's a nice, under-stated outdoor memorial, with a guest book for visitors to sign. Archaeology students regularly conduct fieldwork on the tent-colony site, often finding artifacts and remains of the terror.

The last time I drove by the Ludlow landmark I also looked for the ghost of Drop City, one of the more notorious and long-lasting experimental communes of the 1960s and 70s. I had spent a couple of nights there in 1969 en route to San Francisco to drop off a driveaway car I was transporting from Dallas. The permanent residents of Drop City were accustomed to serving as a counter-culture Holiday Inn; without a fuss, they fed me, gave me a loft and a sleeping bag, and said good-night.

Drop City was a hodgepodge of Buckminster Fuller-style geodesic domes made of two-by-fours and rusty car hoods, situated among chickens and goats on a sloping field outside Trinidad. It had received gobs of international publicity as the first countryside hippie commune, and the reports always spoke of free love and abundant drugs. I didn't see much of either, perhaps because I had a vomitous reaction to my first night's dinner. I spent the next day in bed, ingesting garlic cloves—which, I was assured by an Earth mother from Chicago, would cure me by the following morning. I awoke at sunrise and drove off, still queasy, smelling like a ristra of garlic bulbs. A mining family I knew in the area told me they found the communards curious, but that they paid their bills at the hardware store and politely returned local underage runaways.

I cannot explain why I am attracted to Southwestern mining camps and their stories. Traveling through the towns where America's copper, zinc, and coal originates, I've found a genuine kinship with miners and their families. Certainly it cannot be envy: I have no desire to descend hundreds of feet underground and extract ore or calibrate explosives in a shaft, nor do I want to drive mammoth yellow equipment on tires three times the size of a pickup truck. It cannot be common background, either: The mining communities and I have no shared past. Still, time and again I have been invited into miners' homes and been privileged to listen to family histories and collective memories, to hear cherished songs explained and to read unpublished letters. It's been an honor—one-sided, as far as I can determine—and I've benefited by it enormously.

III. THE OCCIDENTAL TSURIS

Douglas, Arizona, part of the Free State of Cochise, was a copper town, yes, but its other identities grew out of its location along the border and as a ranching center. Like most mining camps, ranching centers, and border towns, it had never been considered a center of Jewish activity. Although El Paso, Texas—and to a lesser extent Nogales on the Arizona-Mexico border—had notable Jewish merchants among their early settlers, Douglas had so few that you could name them all in a minute and still have time for a kosher dill. When author Jeanne Williams learned that the abandoned Jewish cemetery on the eastern edge of Douglas was past deterioration, she set in motion a sequence of activities that culminated in the April 1993 rededication of the small graveyard.

I remember that the ceremony took place on an unusually hot day, but what I recall most was my discomfort at hearing one speaker's pride at the role local Jews had played in the settling of Cochise County. "One Jew was an Arizona Ranger and fought the Indians; another was a sheriff's deputy." Considering the roles played by Arizona's Rangers and the county sheriff back then, this was hardly something to brag about. The Rangers had worked at the behest of mine owners as union-busters and strikebreakers, as had some sheriff's deputies; some Rangers once ventured into Sonora, Mexico to break up a strike. Rangers had also hunted down cattle rustlers for ranchers.

Today the cemetery looks lonely out in the desert scrub just 100 yards from Agua Prieta, Mexico, but it is obviously well cared for. Of the dozen or so headstones still remaining, the earliest notes

Nathan Cohen, born in 1852, and the most recent Bess Dionne Ilitzky Shapiro, who died in 1963. A plaque at the entrance says, "In memory of Jewish pioneers of Cochise County."

Lee Johnson, a Douglas native and genealogist, walked me around the graveyard, then invited me over to the Cochise County Historical Society building at Tenth Street and D Avenue. "Look at this," he said as we stood in the kitchen. He pointed to a full-size wine barrel labeled "Kosher Port." It was addressed to a Rabbi Blumenthal, and Johnson believed that it dated from the early 1920s. He looked in the city directory from that era. "Well, in 1918 Douglas had a Blumenthal Soda Shop."

Across the line in Agua Prieta, the last Jew died in 1996. His name was Kafka. A refugee from Nazi Europe who had settled in Agua Prieta in the early 1940s, Kafka owned a furniture store on Pan American Avenue at Second Street. "He was a prominent merchant and well liked," a Mexican chemist who remembered him told me. "He was one of the few businessmen who sold on the installment plan, so people who couldn't normally afford new furniture could buy from him. He taught me how to play chess when I was a little boy." Today, neither genealogist Johnson nor I know of any Jewish residents in either Douglas or its mirror, Agua Prieta.

～

For a number of years beginning in the late 1970s, I was a stringer for the national desk of the *New York Times*. They asked me to report conventional stories such as court cases, regional angles on

national trends, and curious university research, but what assignment editors valued most was stories pitched from the field—all
the more so, I discovered, if they evoked the Old West with dirt
roads, dusty boots, and barbed wire. Their notion of the Southwest
was matched by my compulsive attempts to fulfill it, and soon, in
deference to my editors, I put a sign over my typewriter: "Remember: Cowboys amble, businessmen stride, mariachis stroll."

One day I learned about a Yaqui Indian who had helped a
Jewish retirees' club unearth an old Jewish graveyard at Boothill
Cemetery in Tombstone. The rededication ceremony was to take
place later that week. This Old West story from Cochise County
linked Jews, cowboys, and Indians—a threefer! Instead of the usual
follow-up questions, I was enthusiastically green-lighted with an
open-ended word count and a photographer.

The Tombstone Hebrew Association had operated during the
legendary city's silver-mining era in the last two decades of the
19th century. "The first thing groups like this would do is conduct
High Holy Day services and establish a burial ground," Harriet
Rochlin, coauthor of *Pioneer Jews: A New Life in the Far West,* told
me. A Tombstone business directory from the 1880s reveals Jewish
surnamed residents in professions such as miner, merchant, banker,
grocer, gunsmith, and restaurant owner. Others were peddlers who
drifted through town after the California gold rush. Most were
first-generation immigrants, including Irish-born gunslinger Jim
Levy, who lived in Tombstone a spell and who, according to
Pioneer Jews, "survived an estimated sixteen shoot-outs before he
was gunned down himself." A Jewish mine superintendent,

Abraham Emmanuel, served as the town's mayor during its declining years, 1896 to 1900.

None of this was known to vacationing Israel Rubin when he and his family visited Tombstone from back East in 1982. A local historian they met casually mentioned that a long-abandoned Jewish graveyard adjoined the infamous Boothill Cemetery, a tourist trap where some of the town's more notorious personalities are said to lie. Together with the historian and their host, Judge C. Lawrence Huerta, the Rubins made their way through catclaw and thick underbrush until they arrived at the crumbled remains of an adobe wall. "That's it," the historian told them, pointing to a small patch of desert scrub facing the Dragoon Mountains. No gravestones remained.

Rubin immediately said Kaddish, the Jewish prayer for the dead, and mused about the possibility of restoring the site for the public. Moved by the scene, Huerta—a Yaqui Indian who had served as a judge and community college administrator—volunteered to help carry out Rubin's vision. The Jewish Friendship Club of Green Valley, the retirement community 100 miles west of Tombstone, soon got into the act, and the operators of Boothill Cemetery lent a hand as well.

Eighteen months later, Rubin and Huerta walked to the same burial ground, this time in the company of 250 of us gathered to celebrate the restoration of Tombstone's Jewish cemetery. We listened as Kaddish was recited once again, only now through a bullhorn by a retired Army rabbi from Sierra Vista, 25 miles west. The 50-by-50-foot cemetery, surrounded by a new wrought-iron fence, had as its centerpiece a two-tier pedestal made of rock from nearby silver mines. Ceremonial items were sealed inside a burnished safe adorned with Jewish and Indian symbols atop the pedestal. These included a yarmulke, a menorah, a Kaddish cup, prayer books and hymnals, and an Israeli bowl filled with soil from Jerusalem. Nacho Montijo, the workman who constructed the pedestal, donated his trowel.

"Why a full-blooded Indian would want to associate with a bunch of Jews," joked the head of the newly formed nonprofit Tombstone Historical Jewish Graveyard, Inc., "is the unanswered question of the hour." For his part, Judge Huerta donated a Yaqui bowl containing prayer sticks, deerskin, Apache tears, and corn pollen. Wearing both an Indian headband and a yarmulke over his long braided hair, Huerta said, "In honoring my Jewish brothers I feel I am also honoring the lost and forgotten bones of my own people, who lay where they fell when the West was being settled." He referred to the dedication ceremony as his own Bar Mitzvah. As a rabbi from Tucson chanted the closing prayer, a slight breeze blew in from the Dragoons.

Every year the Green Valley group, which has since evolved into Temple Beth Shalom, drives over to Tombstone for a memorial service and to say Kaddish at the cemetery. When health permits, Judge Huerta comes too. Under new management, the Boothill gift shop no longer sells $25 "limited edition" pewter replicas of the monument.

∾

A forgotten cemetery along the border. A Yiddish gunslinger in Tombstone. And now, Jewish prisoners in Douglas. If it's not one thing, it's another. Call it the woes of the West, or the occidental tsuris. Few have known that better than Ayla Grafstein.

Ayla was feeling upbeat when we spoke. As far as I could tell, Rabbi Grafstein was always upbeat. She was describing her tenure as a circuit rider making the rabbinical rounds through the Arizona state prison system. From her residence near Mesa, a Phoenix suburb, her drive to the state's lockups in southeast Arizona took her over to Safford and Fort Grant, then Douglas and Tucson, on to Florence, and finally back home. This monthly three-day, 550-mile loop carried Rabbi Grafstein through the San Carlos Indian Reservation; then through the state's cotton-growing region and some splendid backcountry in the Coronado National Forest and the Aravaca Valley; south past the Willcox Playa into pecan- and chile-growing country in the Sulphur Spring Valley; and finally north through the Mule Mountains, past Tombstone and Saint David, and into Tucson before heading up through Oro Valley and onto the Pinal Pioneer Parkway over the Tom Mix Wash. On the fourth day, she rested.

Grafstein was Canadian by birth, Jewish by faith, and an activist by inclination. The Board of Rabbis of Greater Phoenix had a contract with the Arizona Department of Corrections to supply a rabbi to drop in on all the facilities, and Rabbi Grafstein had moved to Arizona in the late 1980s to take the two-year job. Her regular trips to minister to the spiritual needs of Jewish inmates brought her to each of the state's fourteen prisons, where she visited with every inmate who wrote "Jewish" on the "religious preference" line of the prison system's intake form. Of almost 24,000 inmates in mid-2000, 70 had done just that.

"We were up against a lot," recalled Grafstein. "I helped the inmates in Douglas fight an effort to install a cross as a permanent religious symbol in the chapel. All the release programs were Christian-based. A Christian radio station donated equipment to the Department of Corrections if they agreed to broadcast Christian programming. The chaplains in the facilities were all Christians, never Muslim or Native American. All the non-Christians were contract chaplains."

For Rabbi Grafstein, who is part of the Jewish renewal movement, these trips were never easy. "The resident chaplain would go from unit to unit, notifying the Jewish inmates that I was coming. Sometimes Native Americans and Mexicans would attend our services. Catholics were really into them, too. I think they liked the ritual. One inmate got busted for being multireligious: He'd show up for Sunday mass for a sip and come to the Jewish services every month, too. The Muslims sought my help, but they didn't attend my services. We had anywhere from 25 to 40 show up.

"Kosher food became a problem. The inmates weren't happy with their meals. To discourage them from keeping kosher, the prison would order a case of the same precooked meals and feed the inmates the exact same food every meal. They were shipped in from New York."

Committing the same mistake of stereotyping Jewish inmates made by everyone else that I've mentioned the subject to, I asked, "What were they mainly in for, embezzling?"

"No," the rabbi countered. "Drugs. White-collar crimes besides embezzling. One fellow had burned the Jewish community in Phoenix on some investments. He felt good about it. He told me his money was hidden in offshore banking. I asked him, 'What do you tell your kids?' He got a tear in his eye. It was the only time he showed any remorse. Mainly the Jewish inmates were dopers who said they screwed up and wanted to get their lives back together.

"At one Passover meal in Florence we talked about the feeling of liberation and what it takes to get to that place. Even the guards were into it. They said, 'Take as long as you like.' I never had a minyan there except for that Seder. It was the highest Seder in my life."

I attended a Seder at the Arizona state prison at Douglas once myself. Joan Werner, owner of a Bisbee book and music store, invited me and a few others to arrange a Seder. Emily, the owner of an Italian deli in Bisbee, put together the kosher food, Joan supplied the prayer books, and the rest of us kibbitzed. Guards looked on with curiosity and the inmates with envy as we carried basket after basket of food, grape juice, and paper plates into a meeting room. A half-dozen Jewish inmates greeted us, among them an Israeli who conducted the ceremony. "The recalcitrant Hebrews who left Egypt so long ago were rebellious to the point of criminality," said Avi, who had been inside for 12 years. "The promised land I seek is any place outside of prison." We had a marvelous time, we visitors and our hosts.

Many years passed before I went again. Joan Werner invited me once more to accompany her on a Friday-night trek to the prison at Douglas. She had studied Hebrew in her youth and could recite prayers and chant songs at the drop of a yarmulke. The prison system lists some 650 "religious volunteers," including Joan, as eligible to come on site and give spiritual support to inmates. We passed a few security checks and waited for guards to strip-search and escort the Jewish population of the Arizona State Correctional Facility at Douglas to the Mohave Unit visitation room. Fifteen minutes later, two of the 2,200 inmates walked in. It was the lowest turnout Joan had experienced in her many years as a religious volunteer.

The elder of the two, about 60, wore a small knitted yarmulke and a long gray ponytail. He carried a hand-sewn prayer shawl in a handsome cloth bag. The younger, under 30, had short red hair and a neatly trimmed beard but none of the accoutrements of Judaism, symbolic or otherwise. Both wore prison-orange uniforms, the object of much discussion around the yard. Orange uniforms were now mandatory for all prisoners, a change in policy that upset the inmates. After a round of introductions, we chatted about our Judaism.

"I'm an agnostic Jew because I question everything," the elder inmate said.

The younger acknowledged that he had no Jewish background; in fact, he had been raised in a Christian family that took the Bible quite literally. "The more I got to thinking, I realized that if you take the Bible at its word, then we are all Jews. So I put 'Jewish' down on my intake form. I forgot about it until a couple of months later, a guard called me over to tell me to be ready to see the rabbi later that day."

I told them I'd recently located an old reel-to-reel tape of my Bar Mitzvah, but I was reluctant to play it because I still remember the embarrassment of my voice cracking as I read my part of the ceremony.

"I got to lunch late one day," continued red-hair, "and the only seat available was at a table in the back. It turned out to be the Aryan Brotherhood's table. I was invited over by a guy that I know is Jewish but hides it. Afterwards one of the brotherhood came over to my house and asked me if I was Jewish. He said, 'Don't you ever sit at our table again.' A few weeks later, one of the brotherhood guys was taking care of a cat. I had some leftover tuna, so I gave it to him for the cat. Not long after that I had a kitty litter basket and gave that to him, too. He asked if I was Jewish, then said, 'Don't you ever come around to my house again.'" Red-hair was in for drugs and counterfeit currency.

Ponytail: "I was part of a class-action suit against the prison system over shaving regulations. I had a beard. When I refused to shave it, they shackled me and put me in solitary. I eventually shaved it; otherwise I would have been in the hole for my entire 28 years. I felt good when the case went to federal court in Phoenix because the judge was Jewish, but we lost. A Jewish judge ruled against us! Can you believe that?" He preferred not to say why he was in, only that 30 of the 33 charges against him were false.

Red-hair's religious identity led us into a philosophical discussion of just what constitutes a Jew. "My mother was an Armenian Jew and my father was Swede," ponytail volunteered. "I was circumcised at 18 and Bar Mitzvahed at 22."

"The only thing the Torah asks you to believe," Joan said, "is that there is only one God. The rest is how you should live."

We turned in our prayer books to page 269 for your basic Sabbath service. Joan was a terrific lay rabbi. She read the Hebrew, paused on occasion to explain Talmudic nuance, encouraged us to read along with the boilerplate prayers, and kept up a tidy pace that neither indulged nor flouted convention. I looked up when we read God's prescription for dealing with prisoners and the homeless — "Bring freedom to the captive and keep faith with those who sleep in the dust" — but no one else reacted. We closed with a couple of songs in Hebrew whose phonetic sequence I vaguely remembered from childhood. They were nicely transliterated in our prayer books.

The previous day one of Joan's bookstore customers had given her five dollars to buy some chocolate cookies for the inmates. "He does this every month — and he's not even Jewish." She bought the cookies at a new bakery called the Grateful Bread and, together with some juice, served them at the kiddush, the post-service snack. We discussed whether cookies so sinfully rich could still be considered Jewish food, and unanimously agreed that they could. I ran into the gentile cookie-provider a couple of days later and asked him why he did it. "I felt like doing a good thing," he said, looking slightly embarrassed. "It doesn't make any sense."

Of course it does. He had performed high-level *tzedaka*—an act of righteousness in which neither the giver nor the receiver is aware of the other's identity.

IV. AW, SHUCKS

John Kuehn had the only job in the Free State of Cochise that I ever truly wanted. He drove the county bookmobile. John had owned a bookstore in Rockford, Illinois, where he lived in a farmhouse with his wife, Grace. "Our driveway was covered with snow four months of the year. One day in 1978 Grace and I said to hell with it," and they joined the Sunbelt migration. Once they settled in Bisbee, Grace sold real estate and John opened a used- and rare-book shop on Brewery Gulch. He applied for the bookmobile job on a whim. All you really had to know to be the bookmobile driver was how to shift gears on a four-speed GMC Step Van, so the county library staff was delighted when John sought the job: Not only could he drive, but he knew all about books.

I accompanied him one day as he began his route at Barrow's Trailer Park on Highway 80: "The yucca are starting to bloom," a Mrs. McCauley remarked as she handed John a stack of books to reshelve. "I saw a snake in the road this morning," she continued, looking over the romance novels. "First of the season." Before leaving, she asked for a book about the structural geology of the Santa Rita Mountains.

We went on to Saint David and parked in front of the Church of Jesus Christ of Latter-day Saints. A couple in their early 20s drove up and asked for library cards. "We were just passing through from Ohio a few days ago," the wife said, "and we liked it here. We're job hunting now, but one of the first things we wanted to do was get library cards."

John handed them a pen and a form to fill out. "We like to get as many people as possible. That way we can go to the Board of Supervisors at budget time and tell them we've got 6,000 new voters signed up." A teenager walked across the highway to return a book about the Tet offensive. He borrowed a copy of *Catch-22*.

Back in 1981, school authorities in the same town had removed John Steinbeck's *Of Mice and Men* and Joseph Conrad's *Lord Jim* from the reading list of a high-school English class. It wasn't exactly a defining moment in the cultural life of the Free State of Cochise, but it did upset a lot of people. A friend described a subsequent meeting in Saint David about the local high-school curriculum: "They were considering a particular text on U.S. history. Someone had gone through it very carefully, making a note each time there was a reference to women, and brought it up at the meeting. 'Women belong in the home,' she said. 'Not in history.' And they rejected the book."

"It's a funny thing about these communities," John commented as he drove to the local schoolyard. "You can never tell why one type of book is popular at one place and another is popular just a few miles away. In McNeal, wildlife books are very big. But in Double Adobe, war books are in demand."

By day's end county residents had taken out 137 books to enjoy, and in its parking space next to the old high school in Bisbee, the bookmobile rumbled to a halt.

His bookmobile job appealed to me mightily, but what drew me to John was his bookstore. It was stocked with case after case of good, solid literature, back to the 1940s. Each shelf had three or four books that compelled me to pull them down. As I thumbed through each one John, seated at his desk up front, would give me a rundown on its contents, its literary strengths, and its author's life. He seemed intimate with his entire stock. Often I would walk in and simply chew the fat for a while; when the conversation lulled, he would turn around in his swivel chair and pull a book from his rolltop desk. "Here," he'd say, handing me the volume. "I thought you might be interested in this."

It was uncanny. Two times out of three it was a book I'd been seeking for ages but had never told him about, or one that I'd never heard of before—but had to own once he showed it to me. John possessed the finest qualities of a bookseller: He knew his customers and sought out books to their liking without their knowledge. His books brought high prices, and they were worth it. He never printed a catalog, but he did a substantial mail-order business and kept an equal number of books at home, ready to shelve at the store when space allowed. John and I got in the habit of playing Sunday-morning tennis at Vista Park in nearby Warren, where he lived; usually he beat me. I looked forward to these bookstore visits and Sunday tennis matches so much that I would often call ahead to make sure he was available. In retrospect, Dr. Freud, I think it had something to do with my father, an incessant reader and sometime tennis player whom John somewhat resembled.

My addiction to the bookstore on Brewery Gulch intensified when David Eshner, like John a former librarian and bookstore owner, moved to town and opened up another secondhand store in the adjoining storefront. The two stores shared the same front door, there was no divider between them, and they were laid out similarly, so a casual visitor would logically conclude that it was one store. When one owner went out for coffee, the other would often spell him. David's stock was quite different, though, and his strength was literature from and about Latin America, where he had traveled extensively. The stores complemented each other and I felt utterly at ease in both.

David had a comfortably activist bent. In addition to running the store, he worked as a translator (and likewise beat me at tennis with his vicious serve). One day he motioned me toward the back of his store, reached over to lift a trapdoor, and led me down to a basement that few people knew existed. He turned on the light and explained his grand fantasy: converting the basement into a sort of Latin American literary/guerrilla/cultural/linguistic coffee-house—*una tertulia literaria donde se brinda café*. He did have one event, a screening of an irritatingly propagandistic Sandinista video. Not long thereafter, a woman took a tumble down the stairs, broke some bones, and of course sued. So much for the tertulia.

John Kuehn was content to hold literary conversations at his desk, often commenting on this author who had recently visited or that one who had found his or her own book in the store. A few times he suggested I meet a local writer who supported himself washing dishes at a greasy Chinese restaurant on Brewery Gulch.

I begged off, figuring this to be yet another intense Bisbee wanna-be writing his first novel, *Jiggle the Handle*. Later I learned it was Michael Blake, writing *Dances with Wolves*.

In 1988 David and John, both in their early 60s, died of cancer within six months of each other. I indulged my own fantasy and considered buying their stock, moving full-time to Bisbee and becoming a book dealer. Too many practical reasons weighed against it, though, and I soon abandoned the idea.

Walter James Swan had no such inhibition about running a bookstore. Swan, a semiliterate author of no repute, had nothing to lose. Born near Bisbee ten months before the famous deportation, Swan had dropped out of school after eighth grade, eventually married, and raised a family. The Swans lived in California and Arizona, where Walter had a succession of jobs as a bus driver, rail-road brakeman, wartime shipyard worker, beekeeper, janitor, and most of all a plasterer. Although he couldn't write much more than his name, Walter had a soft, magical quality that enraptured listeners as he told simple stories of the old days, recollections of his boyhood, and anecdotes about adventures with his slightly older brother, Henry. The tales began as bedtime stories for his eight children. Having done a miserable job of writing them down, Swan enlisted his wife, Deloris, to type them out. Deloris excised the more egregious punctuation, spelling, and grammatical errors, but like a good editor she preserved the author's singular, simple voice.

Finally, with the kids grown and gone and the two of them on Social Security, the Swans took on his long-held dream of pub-lishing the stories. Because the collection drew on Walter and his brother as kids, they called the book *"me 'n Henry."* Untutored and unagented, they sent the manuscript off to the likes of Knopf and Little, Brown and Company, where it languished in slush piles until form rejections came back. They paid the Scott Meredith Literary Agency $250 to appraise the manuscript. "It doesn't constitute a salable piece of work," came the reply.

What would you do if you had scant literary ability and everybody recognized it? From their doublewide in Palominas, a little west of Bisbee, Walter and Deloris Swan did what far younger independent filmmakers do: They used up their savings, maxed out their credit cards, and mortgaged their property. Deloris taught herself desktop publishing on a new computer and printed out the stories on a new laser printer; the couple then paid a big-city firm to publish the book and bind it in hardback. Walter started selling the 287-page tome at swap meets and county fairs, eventually renting space at the Boothill Cemetery in Tombstone.

A typical opening paragraph:

> *One day Daddy hitched up old Buck to the wagon and he and Mama went into town. They left me 'n Henry at home to look after our little sister, Hazel. It seemed to me that they were gone for hours and we kept a watching towards the top of the hill for them to get back home. You see, the house was in a little valley and the road towards town had to go up over a hill.... [They] returned in a Model T. Me 'n Henry were ready to go any time it was.*

Most of these stories of daily life in rural poverty take up two or three pages and close with an aphorism or moral. Concludes one, quoting his father: "'Walter, there is always a way to solve all problems if you keep your head about you.'" Another ends: "Don't envy what the other fellow has. It may not be as good as what you have."

Sales were pretty good, actually—a dozen a day or more—but it wasn't the book that sold, it was Walter. He wore a black Stetson over a thick mane of white hair, faded denim bib overalls over a white shirt, Western boots, and a slightly shy grin that said, "Aw, shucks."

It was the "Aw, shucks" that did it. Walter Swan was a great aw-shuckser—the best aw-shuckser the Free State of Cochise had ever known.

About this time the novelist T. Coraghessan Boyle, in an interview with the Denver literary journal *Bloomsbury Review,* said, "I'd like to have all the bookshops in America devoted exclusively to my books." Did Walter Swan read that, or was it mere coincidence? Regardless, Swan rented a storefront on Bisbee's Main Street, hung out a shingle of sorts, and began selling the heartwarming *"me 'n Henry."* He called his place the One-Book Bookstore.

Walter Swan's store was met locally with equal parts incredulity, snickers, and curiosity. His furnishings consisted of a comfortable recliner for him to lean back in, a few metal folding chairs for customers, and stacks of *"me 'n Henry."* As if anyone needed proof of how poorly he had performed in school, Walter tacked his eighth-grade report card to the wall: He had received a D- in library, Fs in spelling, geography, and hygiene, and a B in phys. ed.

The One-Book Bookstore opened in the fall of 1989. Within a year, Walter had appeared on half a dozen national television programs, as well as in *People* and a dozen other magazines. David Letterman brought him to New York; Scott Simon visited him in Bisbee. The gimmick—or genius, if you will—was the sheer simplicity of it all. A public relations firm would have undoubtedly botched the Swan account; only Deloris and Walter could pull it off with such unadorned authenticity.

The denizens of Bisbee would peek in the storefront as they walked down Main Street to see how this utterly incongruous merchandising approach was succeeding. Cards and letters came in from all over the world; the Swans posted them on the wall next to one of Walter's original handwritten stories from 1951, replete with elementary errors.

Deloris—a cheerful, heavyset woman who usually wore a sack dress—oversaw the business end of the Swan empire. It was Walter who had the uncanny ability to draw passersby into the store. He would strategically post press clippings about himself in the front window, then pounce on people who slowed to read them.

Chatting with him one time, I noticed some tourists glancing over. I nodded in their direction and offered to leave the room so Walter would have it to himself, much as one might tactfully withdraw when a roommate has a date coming over. "No, no. Not yet." We continued talking, and I thought he was going to lose these potential customers. "This is a game I play with myself. I wait until they have a certain look on their faces. I've got this thing figured out pretty good. It's body language. I'm scoring just about 90 percent." Pause. "OK, *now!* Watch this." Walter stood up, straightened his hat, and lumbered out the door.

"You folks lookin' to learn about that book? Come on in, I'll tell you a story about it." Startled to see the six-foot man whose two-inch pictures lined the window, the tourists followed him inside, not quite knowing what to expect. "I worked hard all my life to be a good husband and father," Walter told them good-naturedly. "I got so old I couldn't work hard anymore, and with the help of my good wife I was able to do something that was a life-long dream."

As he talked, he slowly tore the shrink-wrap off a fresh $19.95 copy of *"me 'n Henry."* Within three minutes Walter had sold and inscribed that copy, wrapped his arms around the visitors for a Polaroid, and invited them to sign the guest book (which doubled as a mailing list for announcements of subsequent self-published volumes about the kindnesses we should bestow on one another). For tourists, it was like a tame ride in a small-town amusement park. "We sure get a lot of warm fuzzies from this book," Deloris said.

Deloris also tended to Walter's clothes. "He's always worn overalls, but now it's important that they be faded. When I buy him some new ones, I have to keep washing them until they look just right."

Jokes in Bisbee about the store soon died out as gallery owners and other local businesses noticed a new breed of customer: Tourists who traveled to this village in the mountains with Walter Swan's One-Book Bookstore as their destination. Bisbee, known for years as off-the-beaten-path, was inching onto that path, and mainstream America was responding. A large roadside billboard on Highway 80 just east of Benson featured Walter and his store. Full-bodied Winnebagos precariously negotiated Old Bisbee's narrow streets. Chartered tourist buses arrived with daytrippers from Phoenix and farther afield.

Walter, for his part, started patronizing the resolutely vegetarian food co-op. He began to wear Birkenstocks instead of cowboy boots. The chamber of commerce declared a Walter Swan Day. Cowboy-turned-realtor Jim Burnett, another local old-timer who had self-published his recollections of "the good old days," tried the same gambit with his own one-book store, but he had too much education—and too little aw-shucksitude.

Walter saw himself on a par with other authors, and why not? "Tom," he said once when I dropped in to see my colleague early one afternoon, "it's just amazing. I've already sold 20 today. I just can't figure it out." He tapped a stack of 20-page illustrated book-lets, each one a children's story he had written. "I give 'em away to the kids. It guarantees that their parents buy the big book. Every time. I've put $3,500 in the bank since the beginning of this month alone." It was the 13th of the month. "That's more than a best-selling novelist makes." Brother Henry, a tax accountant who had recently moved back to Bisbee from Stockton, California, dropped by. He was enjoying the residual celebrity his brother's success afforded him.

Just then a middle-aged couple from Oklahoma walked in and Walter sprang up. "It's a fun book," he offered, in answer to their unasked question. "No bad words. No big words. All true stories. It's about growing up here in Bisbee. A Tom Sawyer book." He was his own best reviewer. "It's a philosophical approach to life." The couple looked at his report card. Deloris offered, "He always said if he couldn't be the best he was going to be the worst. He'd write, 'He threw the cow over the fence some hay.' "

"Eighth grade. That's all the further I went. Ain't that right, Henry?" Henry nodded.

Triple-teamed by Deloris, Walter, and Henry, the poor Oklahoma couple gamely bought a copy. A few minutes later they returned for another.

"Heck," said Walter, "all the distributors wanted 50 percent, and the bookstores got most of the rest. I was going to end up with 5 percent. This way I get it all. It's the easiest thing in the world. Every library in the state's got a copy now. Of course," he confided, author to author, "it don't do me no good, them reading it at the library." He paused. "Well, then again it does. This lady come in and bought one after she read it at the library."

Walter had an ulterior motive for talking to me, and it surfaced every so often. "Tom, I read some of your writing. Why don't you write me up? I just know that *Modern Maturity* and *Arizona Highways* would buy something from you in an instant."

He inscribed a book for me: *To Tom, a fello auther.*

When business was slow, Walter would lean back in his chair and snooze a spell, looking much like a Duane Hanson sculpture. At the peak of his popularity in the early 1990s, an enthusiastically bad local theater company staged an original comedy review, plunking an actor in Swan's clothing in a rocker as an on-stage fixture.

Not long after his 78th birthday—by which time he had sold more than 25,000 books—Walter Swan went to bed for the last time. His brother Henry sat in for him at the store, but of course people came for the *me*, not the *Henry*, and book sales fell off. Walter looked peaceful lying in an open casket at the local Mormon church on Melody Lane. His family had the good sense not to dress him in his aw-shucks outfit.

V. AT EASE

We were sitting at the bar of Bisbee's venerable Copper Queen Hotel one Friday evening, Margo and I and a dry-docked sailor friend of hers from the Florida Keys, when a woman a few stools down opened her purse. She looked lethally Scottsdale—every follicle of her frosted hair in place, nice eyeliner, a stylish Ralph Lauren denim outfit, diamond studs in her ears, a diamond tennis bracelet, skin tanned out of season, long maroon nails, and white hightops that dirt dared not touch. Margo and I were teaching her friend how to tell the difference between weekenders from Tucson and those from Phoenix. Margo, a realtor, said, "Half of the couples here are married—"

"But not to each other," I broke in, singing a line from the Tammy Wynette song. "This is where people come for weekend affairs. Look at those two over there." I motioned toward a nicely dressed Chicano couple smooching at a corner table in the shadows. "You know, I admire a man who has the courage to run away from his problems."

That's when Ms. Scottsdale pulled a white cellular phone from her purse, twirled it around like an ivory totem so it reflected the light just right, and whacked it down on the bar. There was dead silence for a moment as we hillbillies adjusted to this obviously sophisticated visitor and tried to absorb her late-20th-century technology. Even Danielle, the bartender, did a double take. "Why can't

I get a connection here?" Ms. Scottsdale demanded of no one in particular as she fondled her phone. "What's wrong with this place?"

Taken literally, her second question was entirely valid; indeed, many of us often dwelled on it at length. But together with her first, well, it revealed what was right with this place. Cellular repeaters had not yet covered the hilly section of Bisbee, and you were plumb out of luck if you wanted to crank up your cell phone there. Until mid-1993, you could still call someone's home simply by dialing a "2" and the last four digits. Even today, people cite only four digits when giving their phone numbers; every phone in town begins with the same exchange. Unless you subscribe to the local cable company, the terrain makes decent radio and television reception impossible (excepting a classical music station relayed from Tucson). The best TV program in town is the weekly City Council meeting, featuring a civically impaired cast playing to a live audience of do-gooders and do-badders alike.

Mass communication means scanning the notices on the bulletin board next to the post office. Despite a mere 6,500 residents, Bisbee has always had three or four newspapers. I recently stumbled across a 1979 issue of the long-since-defunct biweekly *Mule Mountain Observer*, in which I made fun of the local food co-op for apologizing for selling mayonnaise with sugar in it while simultaneously stocking Chiquita bananas, then the focus of a concerted boycott by the United Farm Workers. Margo was telling her sailor-boy about the most recent doomed effort to Aspenize the town when Ms. Scottsdale's weekend paramour returned from the bathroom. Ms. Scottsdale quietly tucked the phone back in her purse.

The Copper Queen Hotel was built in 1902 by the Phelps Dodge Company to house visiting executives and businessmen. Its gingerbread appearance and comfortable front patios lend an ambience that, combined with its durability and reputation, have made it preferred lodging for generations. The Queen bar has catered to its share of eccentrics, wackos, and characters—even encouraged them at times—and on a weekday night you might still find an off-season ski bum from Taos, a faded beauty queen from Midland, or a cyclist from France.

The Queen's bright, high-ceiling restaurant would be a pleasure to dine in if the food was better or the prices lower. The last time I had dinner there, our waitress was the height of Bisbee fashion: goofy baggy pants, a tie-died shirt, oversize plastic glasses, and a pencil in her hair. The service was fine until she brought the check. She had written "God Loves You!" on it. Finding this highly inappropriate, I crossed it out and handed it back in the leather folder with my credit card.

She returned a minute later. "You didn't think I should have written 'God Loves You!' on there?" she asked.

"It did seem out of place, yes." At this she hurled herself across the table and embraced me, crying out, "God is always loving, kind, and merciful. He loves all men!" I managed to untangle myself from her arms and straighten out my shirt. Other diners looked over, then resumed their conversations, pretending nothing had happened.

≈

Bisbee's appeal lies in its satisfaction with making ends meet and the suspicion of anything more grandiose. In this town with its doggedly classless class, quality control and standards took the last stage West. On occasion, a gentrification disturbance threatens and shops become shoppes, but the gathering clouds soon dissipate, the turnover of stores on Main Street continues, and Bisbee retains its reputation as America's only town with a maximum wage.

You may remember the honorable prostitute Lynn Braken, played by Kim Basinger in *L.A. Confidential*. In her seductive boudoir, Lynn kept a throw pillow embroidered with a map of Arizona, with her hometown of Bisbee embroidered on it as well. Her ambition was to take her ill-gotten gains and open a dress shop there. "The women of Bisbee," she purred, "they could use some fashion." At movie's end, the hooker and her cop boyfriend head not into the sunset but east to Bisbee to open up that dress store.

I savor slowly formed friendships with retired miners who sit on the same downtown benches day after day. Two Mexican border towns lie within 25 miles of Bisbee, and I occasionally make the rounds of stores there, picking up white cheese, corn tortillas, and the latest Latin American cassettes. One Saturday night I stopped for a beer at St. Elmo, a dive on Brewery Gulch that dates from 1902. There were six large shiny black motorcycles parked outside. Not far away another bar advertised, "Sexy beer! Sudsy women!"

Brewery Gulch winds back into the hills and further back into history. In its early days it was home to miners in their rooming houses, prostitutes in their cribs, and whole families in cramped quarters. It looked "like a vast amphitheater," wrote Conrad

Richter in *Tacey Cromwell,* his novel about Bisbee at the start of the last century, "with houses hanging like wasps' nests one above the other all around the horseshoe of tall cliffs." Today far fewer homes hang around the horseshoe, and those that remain house families of retired Chicano miners, recent arrivistes who have nicely rehabilitated their homes, and artists who have reason to hide.

Late one afternoon Waldo Barcelo insisted on showing me his home on the Gulch. Waldo was one of Bisbee's chronic homeless, a seldom-mentioned layer of the population with its own historical precedent. He was a level or two below No Visible Means of Support. We met on a bench in Grassy Park across from the old Phelps Dodge Mercantile.

"My Dad worked for P-D. My Mom used to send me over there to buy things with coupons. I used to shine shoes in a bar as a kid. Seven cents a shine. One day I was shining a man's penny loafers and I accidentally got some shoe polish on his white socks. He kicked me right here." He showed me a scar on his forehead.

"I was born here in 1949. Everyone says good morning to me. Everyone waves. No one's afraid of me. They don't know what it's really like. I worked in the open pit as a laborer, then operating the crusher. Then they transferred me to Morenci. Look at me. In high school I ran cross country. Now I can't even walk across town. In the morning I buy a quart of beer and go up on the mountain to drink it. I drink; that's my choice. I buy frozen burritos and leave them out in the sun to thaw. When I bite into them I almost break the few teeth I have left. I got my dinner from a Dumpster last night." He struggled to pull out his wallet with a picture of his young grandson. "I use Super Glue for my glasses, and I put the tube in the same pocket. A little of the glue came out. That's why it's so hard to get my wallet out." When Waldo finally extracted his wallet and displayed the picture of his grandson, he cried.

We strolled over to the Gulch, and Waldo told me a joke about one of the Gulch rats: This fellow is on Brewery Gulch outside St. Elmo when someone empties a .45 into him.

"Bartender, bartender," he cries out as he falls to the sidewalk. "Call the police! I've been shot!"

"You call the police," the bartender replies. "You're the one who's shot, not me."

Waldo slapped his thigh at his own joke and repeated the punch line to himself.

"There," he said, motioning over to the right. "That's where I live." We were about half a mile into the Gulch, but I didn't see any houses where he was pointing. "Right there." He led me over to a couple of abandoned cars in junkyard condition. "This is my home." His home was a rusted gray discarded station wagon parked at an uncomfortable downhill angle, about ten years old, with 140,000 miles on the odometer. "Real sad, huh?" It had a New York State inspection sticker on it, and it had been left here to die. Three of the tires were hopelessly flat; the fourth wheel had no tire at all.

Waldo slept in a tattered, dirty, lightweight blue sleeping bag that lay in the back. One of the windows had been smashed in, and shards of glass lay all around his bed. Empty beer cans and bottles filled the broken seats. Behind his back people called this car the Waldo Astoria. I stuck my head inside the car and recoiled from the stench of stale beer, filthy clothes, and half-empty meat tins. "It gets cold at night when you only have one blanket," was all Waldo would say.

Before we parted, Waldo suggested that I walk over to St. Patrick's and look into the eyes of Saint Teresa. The next day I did just that. She stood on a pedestal about four feet off the ground clutching roses and a wooden cross with Jesus on it. Her face was ivory white, with kindly green eyes looking down. It reminded me of the town's annual Virgin of Guadalupe skit-and-candlelight procession a few years back. The organizers had asked me to play the role of Juan Diego, the Indian campesino whose vision of the Virgin of Guadalupe has led to more than four centuries of Catholic dominance over the Mexican masses. They dressed me in a calf-length cape and we staged it on the steps of the Mining and Historical Museum. I played it straight and satisfied both camps who showed up at the event—the devout Mexicans, candles in hand, and those who saw it as deep kitsch.

What appeals to me most about the capital of the Free State of Cochise, I suppose, is its natural continuity. When the plums and other fruit fall off the trees, it's not uncommon to see javelina snorfing around, chomping them off the ground. In the monsoon season storms rush through the canyons, clouds bouncing back and forth between the mountain walls that define the town's outer limits. It's inspiring to watch the power go out, candles light up, and gullies overflow. At sundown, a stand of backlit tamarisks shuddering in the distance looks like an impressionist painting.

For many years, a drunk who lived up the small side canyon

where I stayed in Bisbee staggered home every night around 11, moaning as he pulled himself uphill. At first my neighbors and I were perplexed; then we were concerned; finally, on hearing the moaner every night, we felt reassured, as if the sound of a far-off foghorn had just reached our ears.

On many Sunday afternoons I joined a game of middle-aged volleyball at Brown Dog Stadium. A pickup truck in the parking lot bore a bumper sticker reading, IF IT'S THE TOURIST SEASON, CAN WE SHOOT THEM? After a hiatus of a few years, the Fourth of July coaster race down Tombstone Canyon has come back. ("THANK'S!" said a sign from the city public works department.) And on the edge of town, the Cochise County Lesbian and Gay Alliance Adopt-a-Highway sign has stood so long that passing yahoos don't even bother to shoot it anymore.

Bisbee has single-handedly put "quaint" and "nestled" back into travel writing, but there's really no reason for industrial tourism: no ski resort, no world-renowned natural formation, no wax museum. Just the other day I saw a notice on the post-office bulletin board; the Ladies' Tea and Terrorism Society was raising funds for a local women's shelter. These days my Bisbee routine includes a midday walk along the winding road downtown to pick up an out-of-town newspaper, drop in on a merchant or two, then sip coffee with the floating crew of NVMSers.

Perhaps that's why I feel at ease here. We speak of this region as the Old West when in fact this quadrant in America's lower left-hand corner was the most recently settled part of the lower 48. This adventurous, once-prosperous copper town near the border lives precariously on a suspension bridge between the two Wests, drawing its stability and independence from both sides.

I've often wondered how my life would be different had I opened a bookstore on Brewery Gulch.

ACKNOWLEDGMENTS

I have good friends and I've had good editors. On occasion the two groups overlap. Their qualities have sustained me, whether wisdom shared or writing encouraged. They have always broadened my perspective and often sharpened my prose.

Each in his or her own way has contributed to the making of this book, and for that I am thankful to the following: James Austin, Christine Brennan, Kim Brown, John Crewdson, Chris Dietz, Marine Dominguez, Mike Enis, George Hawke, Beth Henson, Robert Houston, Laurie Kintzele, Peter Knobler, the late Andrew Kopkind, Tom Kunkel, Michael Lacey, Antonio Lopez, Gregory McNamee, Charles Miller, Michael Miller, Boyd Nicholl, David Quammen, Ron and Elaine Querry, Valerina Quintana, Ray Ring, William Schmidt, Sharon Seymour, Keoki Skinner, Paul Steiner, Tom Stites, Ray Turner, and Ed Ward. My appreciation especially goes to Elizabeth Newhouse for having the foresight to sign up this book, and to Patrice Silverstein for having the insight to improve it.

ABOUT THE AUTHOR

Tom Miller is the author of six previous books, including *Trading with the Enemy: A Yankee Travels Through Castro's Cuba*, *The Panama Hat Trail*, and *On the Border*, and editor of *Arizona: The Land and the People*. His articles have appeared in *Life*, the *New York Times*, *Rolling Stone*, and many other publications. Miller lives in Tucson, Arizona.